WILD

W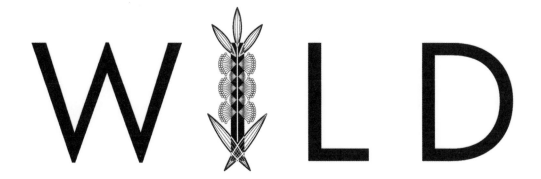LD

....

Plant-based Recipes to
Nourish your Wild Essence

....

JOEL GAZDAR & AISTE GAZDAR
Founders of Wild Food Café

1 3 5 7 9 10 8 6 4 2

Vermilion, an imprint of Ebury Publishing,
20 Vauxhall Bridge Road,
London SW1V 2SA

Vermilion is part of the Penguin Random
House group of companies whose
addresses can be found at global.
penguinrandomhouse.com

Penguin
Random House
UK

Text Copyright © Wild Food Café Un Limited
2019
Photography © Wild Food Café Un Limited
2019

Joel Gazdar and Aiste Gazdar have asserted
their right to be identified as the authors of
this Work in accordance with the Copyright,
Designs and Patents Act 1988

This edition first published by Vermilion
in 2019

www.penguin.co.uk

A CIP catalogue record for this book is
available from the British Library

Design: Two Associates
Project editor: Samantha Crisp

ISBN 9781785042300

Printed and bound in China by C&C Offset
Printing Co., Ltd

Penguin Random House is committed to
a sustainable future for our business, our
readers and our planet. This book is made
from Forest Stewardship Council® certified

CONTENTS

INTRODUCTION

Take a moment to remember the call of birdsong. The smell of fresh blades of grass. The sensation of walking through an enchanting forest. Touching dew drops with your fingertips. Inhaling fresh mountain air deep into your lungs. Soaking your feet in the ocean, your body basking in sunshine. Feeling the spaciousness of your being. Feeling connected. It is inside you. It is your wild essence. Allow it to guide you.

It no longer makes sense to live out of tune with nature. We hear its call; it is inviting us to eat with the seasons, to connect with the wild, to feel the cosmos, to remember, to tune in to the rhythmic wave of life. This call is an invitation to our innate natural state of being and thriving. By recognising that we are part of a bigger whole, we start learning to tune in to it, to navigate it with mastery, and through this process we get to know ourselves deeper and awaken our intuition.

The time we are living in is calling for new ideas, solutions and possibilities to be brought into fruition in an innovative, holistic approach: both nutritionally and environmentally. Acknowledging and celebrating the wild is our way of connecting with the spirit of the Earth – that timeless wisdom that is at the very centre of this book, our food and our work.

The closer we are to nature, by eating fresh, seasonal, raw, wholesome, organic, wild, biodiverse food, the more we reconnect ourselves to the ecosystem and the more responsive and receptive we become.
It's a no-brainer.

The wild inspires us to be dynamic, more natural, to keep learning and to get to know ourselves and our environment beyond what we've ever experienced before, diving deeper into life's unfolding evolution and enjoying the journey. The wild calls us regardless of our urban or rural upbringing, our cultural, social or personal aversion to or fondness for nature and the outdoors. Whether it is a gentle whisper we can barely hear, or a powerful roar that we cannot ignore, it is here. It is a part of us, it is the core of our individual and collective thriving.

Being wild is many things. Simply put, it is living life connected to our essence and to our environment. Wild is the wisdom of a biology of which we are all made. By observing and appreciating all aspects of how magnificently nature works; how inner and outer nourishment affects our bodies, minds and feelings in unique ways, we can learn to harness and reconnect to the wisdom of our wild essence and embody more qualities of it in our lives.

This book is an ode to our devotion and immersion into plant food deliciousness, environments and lifestyle practices for full-spectrum nourishment. We trust it will inspire you in your own holistic journey of playful culinary exploration, investigation and wellbeing. We want to help you to open new and familiar doors of inner and outer discovery, using this book as a compass, a map and an inspiring companion.

Everything we talk about in this book describes a dynamic flow of the elements through ingredients, recipes, rituals and seasonal environments. Allow yourself to be inspired, but don't take it (or yourself) too seriously. Inner thriving won't be found through following rigid rules imposed by someone else. It is about dusting off your inner compass and allowing your wild essence to guide you. Be your own guide but be open to signs and feedback in all forms.

See the practices and recipes that are in this book as doorways into more creativity, deliciousness and thriving. When you feel drawn to a particular practice or recipe, explore and research it further; individualise it to suit you or switch up the ingredients.

The practices and rituals listed in this book are extremely simple, but don't be fooled by their simplicity. Our lives were not meant to be overly complicated. Returning to the simplicity of being, both with food and with our lifestyle, will feel similar to decluttering a wardrobe or tidying up a house. It resets and rebalances our inner and outer environment to the natural rhythms of the wild. We and the wild will start sharing the same breath again.

In this modern age we have lost the ability to look at the world around us in a holistic way, and this applies to the way we think about nutrition too, often focusing too heavily on certain ingredients or studying nutrition by stripping everything down to isolated nutrients. Our approach and commitment is to bring holistic understanding back into the study and application of nourishment, and to celebrate it as the art, craft and science of ourselves, our relationships and our environment.

JOEL AND AISTE

Between the two of us, we have over 30 years of personal experience in integral practices of wellbeing, including raw food, herbalism, nutrition, astrology, yoga and other holistic movement and personal development practices. We both benefited immensely from switching to a plant-based way of eating in our late teens.

We have been fortunate enough to travel in all four directions and have been apprenticed to many traditional peoples of knowledge from different cultures of the world, from Ayurveda in India, Tibetan and traditional Chinese medicine, European herbalism, African herbalism and the global shamanic cornucopia and plant medicines of South and North America.

Besides having a restaurant and creating some really exquisite, elevated meals over the years (a lot of which you will find in this book), we still maintain that our all-time favourite meals have been wild strawberries foraged in the forest, coconuts opened on the beach, tomatoes picked and eaten straight from the garden, a feast of wild purslane found on the sea shore, cacao drunk by the fire with Mayan elders and durian eaten with our bare hands. That's why whenever we talk about food, we try to strike a balance: super simple meals woven with intricate dining experiences; food made just for ourselves and feasts created with an intention of sharing; food prepared by someone else and that made by ourselves.

In our lifelong immersive exploration of food and wellbeing styles from around the world, we intentionally chose a path less trodden. We celebrate and specialise in those natural plant foods, ingredients, practices and methods that haven't been fully appreciated and explored, or haven't received as much attention as the current go-to everyday staples. We are not caught up in the reasons why one should or shouldn't be vegan or plant-based. To be perfectly honest, we are not that fond of the 'V' word, because of the polarised emotion that it provokes. Wellbeing and thriving is about so much more than what that concept can convey. Simply put, we choose to eat in a way that causes the most benefit and least suffering to the inhabitants of the Earth, and in a way that is the most nourishing, fun, delicious and empowering to us. Other than that, we choose to let the deliciousness of the food and the wisdom of the wild vibe do the talking.

WILD FOOD CAFÉ

The cultural pioneer and spiritual teacher Ram Dass once asked his teacher, the Indian mystic Neem Karoli Baba, how he could perpetuate more enlightenment. His teacher answered, 'Feed people'.

We opened Wild Food Café in 2011, when raw and plant-based cuisine was still very much at the fringes of popular culture and the media. Our dream was to make it an oasis of delicious plant food and wellbeing in the centre of the city.

We miraculously experienced a series of fortuitous events that meant that within a few months we were the proprietors of a restaurant in the very heart of Neal's Yard, Covent Garden. Wild Food Café soon attracted a loyal following and a solid base of regulars who loved the food we made, the way we made it, and the vibe we'd created – as much as we did. Wild Food Café grew from a small lunchtime-only eatery to two busy restaurants with queues outside the door.

The foods we most loved when we were children still carry an immense emotional connection for us to this day. Naturally, we were keen to recreate the popular, globally inspired dishes that so many of us have an emotional connection to – burgers, pizza, pasta, falafel, sushi and so on – but using pristine, biodiverse, raw-centric, artisan ingredients, either sourced locally or from the wild zones and ecosystems around the world.

Every dish was meticulously thought through, not only to be totally delicious and tick all the flavour, texture and colour boxes, but also to provide solid nourishment and a medicinal or wild factor. We made everything from scratch, using as many wild, unusual, medicinal spices and superfoods as we could pack into one recipe. In the first few years you would often find us in the kitchen at 1 in the morning peeling a mountain of fresh artichokes for the dinner service the next day, creating yet another batch of wild burger patties, or sorting through the wild edibles that had just been delivered from deepest Wales.

Yet, with all these intense food explorations going on, it was always crystal clear in our hearts from the very beginning that the most important ingredient was the vibe. The love, intent and awareness of the person making and serving the food needs to be shared with the guest receiving it. Our intention was to create a home, a family, a community, an oasis in the centre of town, where good vibes and the plain simple celebration of life are shared by all. This thread is very much at the core of everything we do to this day. A happy fulfilled team will create happy delicious food and provide a nourishing experience to all guests. For us, it has to begin and end with a loving intention, kindness and care, and that's why at Wild Food Café all plates of food are an expression of celebration and appreciation of each one of us: of our community, of our suppliers, our planet, our humanity and everything around us.

WILD WELLBEING PRINCIPLES

THE ALCHEMY OF APPRECIATION

Before we get too carried away with food, we always remind ourselves, as well as our guests, our students and the team, that the first and most important ingredient is our attitude. The attitude of gratitude with which we see the world, ourselves and what's on our plate is the most powerful alchemist tool, free at our disposal at all times. We are incredibly privileged to be able to explore, play with and create using ingredients from near and far; to have access to seasonal, organically grown and wild food; to foster relationships with incredible artisan growers, suppliers and foragers; and have enough to put on our plate every day. We have way more at our disposal than our bodies require to live on, and for this reason and many others, we start every conversation about food with an expression of gratitude. This simple reminder brings us to our hearts.

PLAYFUL AND CONTINUOUS EXPLORATION

Let's remember that we are all soaring in an infinite universe on a giant living spaceship that is planet Earth. Life is a continuous flow of change and transformation, as is our wellbeing and our relationship with food. Even your own centre, your own truth, will always be dynamic and on the move. Whenever we attach ourselves to ready-made static answers we find ourselves struggling against the flowing, evolving, undulating, mysterious paradox of life. When we think we have the answer we close our hearts and minds to the open, delicate vulnerability of the present moment.

There is not one answer that we could, or would want to, ever give to you on what is the right or wrong food to eat. The appropriate food and flavours for us yesterday might not be the perfect food for us today. What is right for us in summer is most likely not going to be suitable for us in winter. We always try to keep ourselves available and open to new possibilities, discoveries, ingredients and techniques; inevitably they always show up!

RESPECT THE CYCLES

While continuous exploration might sound daunting and overwhelming for those looking for steady answers, the cycles of nature and the rhythms of the cosmos hold us in a constant rhythmic, cyclically repetitive flow, giving us an abundance of opportunities to live our lives in the most magical way. Seasons, times of the day, days of the week, moon and sun cycles are our reference grid for when to return to certain ingredients and practices. Think of wild greens, sprouts and asparagus in spring, strawberries in May and June, plums in August, figs in September, grapes in October, wild mushrooms in autumn, roots in winter and so on. In spring, be activated, bright, bubbling and full of inspiration; in summer, be ripe, joyful and overflowing; in autumn, be transformational, abundant, creative and generous; and in winter, be solid, centred, focused, grounded and cosy. Explore the mind-blowing paradox of infinite variety and diversity, unique yet familiar every season.

EMBRACE SELF-CARE RITUALS

You can eat the best food in the world, but if for the rest of the time you are neglecting yourself, your body, mind, emotions, your relationships and your connection to the environment – it is not going to do you much good. Food is only one part of nourishment, and it will never provide an answer to all our questions. Inevitably, all our interactions with the world around us – from the moment we awake to the moment we go to bed – either deplete or nourish us mentally, emotionally, energetically and physically. Ritual practices are simple inner tools that we have at our disposal to hold us centred in our own space, to focus on the states and experiences that are nourishing and beneficial to us. They provide a way to nurture our own essence and connection to the wild in the midst of (often hectic) lives.

Every meal, every breath and every interaction can become a personal self-care ritual. Some of our favourite rituals for increasing presence are dance and other forms of movement, hydration, relaxation, spending time in nature, meditation, freeing the singing voice and other creative expressions, positive affirmation and prayer, family and community participation.

DEVELOP MEANINGFUL, POSITIVE RELATIONSHIPS WITH EVERYONE AND EVERYTHING

For us it is not so much the food per se that is important, but the relationships – both inner and outer – that food fosters. It can take us down many cultural memory lanes, it holds the food and lifestyle memories of our parents, grandparents, ancestors and cultures. It also holds with it the ability to return to a harmonious, present-moment-based relationship with ourselves and the environment that is unique, dynamic, playful and empowering. Adopting a more conscious approach to ourselves, our relationship with food, and all our relationships is the only way to transform from a segmented and disconnected consumer culture into a thriving and productive collaboration.

CELEBRATE EVERYTHING!

Once we have the attitude of gratitude, we might as well celebrate everything and practise continually remembering how lucky we are. When life throws us a curve ball we see it as either a blessing or a blessing in disguise. To help you practise this attitude ask yourself the question, 'which blessings and benefits can I be open to perceiving in this situation or challenge?' Write as many answers as you can on paper until your emotional vibrational state is uplifted. This principle is the backbone of full-spectrum nutrition and invariably nourishes all relationships – with food and beyond.

WILD

WELLBEING

COMPASS

FULL-SPECTRUM NOURISHMENT

The four elements
are the core basic recipe
of which all life is made.

In many traditional cultures, the world consists of four elements and corresponding directions: Air – East, Fire – South, Water – West and Earth – North. Often, another three levels are added to signify the multi dimensional nature of our experience: up, down and middle, or the centre. Up represents the skies – sometimes referred to as the heart of the cosmos, down represents the heart of the earth that's below us, and middle represents the centre of our experience – the heart of humanity. These are the basic orientation directions in time and space of all physical forms, all of which lead to and from the centre, here and now, the heart of our own personal compass that is in tune with the natural wisdom of the wild.

The Wild Wellbeing Compass is a symbolic visual representation of seasons, flavours, elements and directions that carry with them complementary seeds of holistic nourishment and balance. By looking at these different parts in context to each other and how they balance as a whole, we can notice the areas where we might be overlooking or ignoring our bodies, minds, emotions or relationships. Learning how to acknowledge and balance all those directions – and corresponding elements – while being in a dynamic state of aliveness, is what turns us into the alchemists of our own thriving and allows the wild essence that is in each one of us to be integrated and activated in our day-to-day lives.

The compass is an invitation to start thinking about and experiencing ourselves and our ability to thrive as a holistic being (in a way that transcends the polarised black/white, good/bad concepts) and access our own innate natural wisdom. It is a reminder that by unifying the body and the mind through the heart, and approaching our lives as a part of the interconnected web of the wild – holistically and naturally – each one of us can sharpen and fine-tune our intuition and understanding about the foods, the tools, the environments, the practices and the elements that we require at each moment to experience our most connected, wild selves.

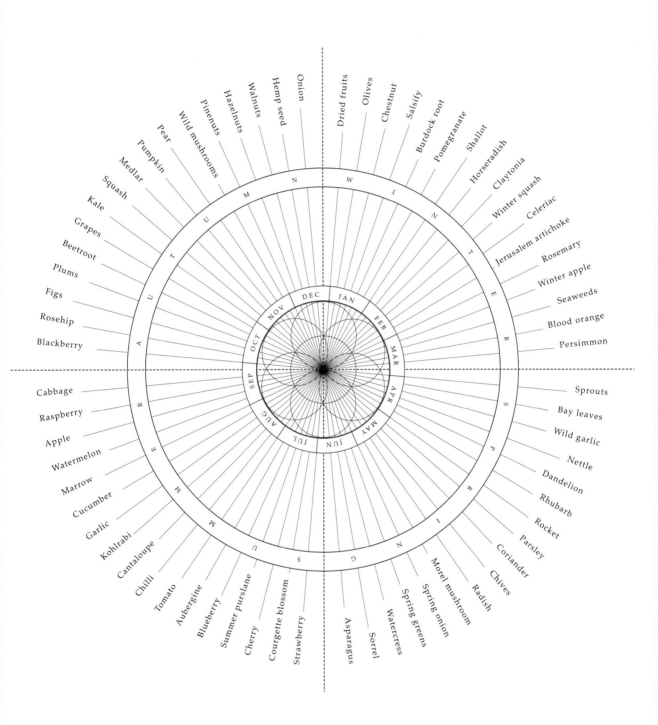

FEELING-BASED BEINGS

We are feeling-based beings. We all know and have the ability to experience different states, whether physical, emotional or mental. We all have the living memory of hot, cold, dry, windy, wet, solid, hard, soft, light and heavy. In a similar way, we all agree on what sadness, anger, frustration, anxiety, depression, happiness, joy, peace and stillness feels like in our bodies. It boils down to the visceral experience of expansion or contraction, openness or closedness, relaxedness or tightness, flow or blockage, comfort or discomfort.

Originally, biologically, and at our deepest essence, the natural tendency for each one of us — beyond learned, practised habits — is to gravitate towards the centre, our heart, the place from which we can have the clearest perspective of the whole. That is what naturally happens to us when we spend longer periods of time in the embrace of the wilderness. Yet, invariably, whenever we get more disconnected from the gentle guidance of nature and become stuck in the concrete jungles of our modern lives — with

square buildings, high-stress environments and standard industrialised diets — we find ourselves wobbling around the peripheries of the compass, leading to excessive challenges and disharmony.

ELEMENTAL ALCHEMY

As we start implementing all the techniques to help us become fluent in our inner language, we notice that our bodies, emotions and feelings tend to be dominated by one or two of the elements. Simply put, air correlates to the mind, fire to the heart, water to the feelings, and earth to the body. If it is air that is dominant, we tend to be very ethereal and dreamy and in stressful situations tend towards anxiety and overwhelm. If it is fire, we tend to be driven, passionate, wilful and enthusiastic with dynamic emotions of courage, anger and frustration. If it is water, we tend to be reflective and empathic, with deep feelings and emotions guiding our way, but imbalances can also lead us into depressive states of feeling too much or not at all. When we are earthy we are practical, focused, grounded, present and resourceful. Whenever out of balance, we might find ourselves with tendencies towards narrow-minded thinking, possessiveness, inertia or laziness. Our internal make-up contains all the elements in proportions that are unique to us, yet there are patterns where different elements dominate different areas of our lives. Once we start becoming aware of the principles of the elements interacting within our bodies and environments (and the qualities, symbols, foods and tools associated with each), then we have at our fingertips infinite recipes and variations according to our unique body, life, time of day and season.

THE ARCHITECTURE OF A DISH

Whenever we share a recipe, we feel it is our responsibility to explain the architecture of the meal. This understanding will empower you to make tweaks and adjustments to take the recipe in any direction that you feel. It also makes it a lot easier to adapt it to your specific location, season and budget.

The quintessential deliciousness of a dish is made up of five main flavours. Some medicinal and culinary cultures have more distinct subcategories of flavour: Ayurveda has the addition of pungent and astringent; Japanese food culture gives us the distinction of an umami flavour as a further shade of savouriness; and the European system has a way of distinguishing tangy and sour. The different flavours complement and balance each other, each one making that dish complete, fulfilling and 'gourmet' but each flavour also contains certain medicinal elements and energetic properties. They might seem conflicting at first glance – depending on which system of knowledge you look into – but they all work together to create a sensational synthesis and harmony of flavour that is both mouth-watering and medicinal.

When you look into it, you will find that 99.9 per cent of the junk foods we are all familiar with are made using mono-agriculturally produced hybridised staple foods, such as wheat, soy, corn, potato, sugar and seedless fruit. By definition these are all starchy grains, fruits and vegetables that are high in sugars and low in mineral content. In the vast majority of cases, wherever the more medicinal components of sour and bitter flavours and their corresponding minerals have been removed, the more it results in bland flavour which then requires the artificial addition of processed salt. The more refined, hybridised foods that we eat, the less we get to experience the medicinal spectrum of whole bitter and sour foods and flavours, foods that come with a multitude of health benefits and are essential for our thriving. Therefore, the more courageously we venture into the spectrum of sour and bitter foods, alongside already familiar salty (umami) and sweet, the better we will feel and the more thriving we can experience.

The components within each flavour group are interchangeable, which gives us room to play and experiment with our own unique combinations. For example, if a recipe calls for apple cider vinegar, we can look around our kitchen to see if we have anything else sour, such as lemon or lime, baobab powder or rosehip, to name a few of the sour fruits. Once we become more comfortable with which foods fit into which categories and how they work together in a complementary way, then we understand how to bring uniqueness and balance to our dishes according to the local area, availability, season and budget – as well as our personal preferences.

THE BUILDING BLOCKS OF FLAVOUR

BITTER FOODS
AIR

All green leafy vegetables, in particular chicory, rocket, watercress, endive, kale and the brassica family, as well as the likes of asparagus, artichoke and radicchio; most citrus fruits (including lemon, lime, orange), although mostly known for their sour properties, can also be bitter, especially in their pith and seeds. Wild greens, especially dandelion and nettles; sprouts and aromatic herbs such as parsley, dill, coriander, thyme and oregano; coffee, tea, medicinal mushrooms; bitter spices such as ginger, galangal, cumin, mustard, fenugreek, aniseed and turmeric. Most vegetables and fruit, especially those with a slight edge of bitterness, such as courgette, squash, cucumber (especially the thin-skinned varieties), aubergine, bitter melon; seaweeds, quinoa, cacao, tahini and sesame seeds.

SOUR FOODS
FIRE

All sour citrus fruits (lemons, limes, oranges); apple cider vinegar; some greens such as sorrel and wood sorrel; all sour berries and their powders (sea buckthorn, camu camu, rosehip, raspberry, strawberry, sour cherries); tamarind, green mango, probiotic and fermented foods and drinks; umeboshi plums, kimchi, kombucha, kefir; nut and seed cheeses, pickles.

SPICY & PUNGENT FOODS
FIRE

Culinary spices, chillies, onion, garlic, ginger, galangal, turmeric, mustard, wasabi, horseradish, leek, radish and radish sprouts, mustard leaf, watercress, brassicas such as cauliflower, cabbage, broccoli and kale, etc.

SWEET FOODS
WATER

All ripe, sweet juicy fruit; tropical fruit, such as papaya, mango and durian; cantaloupe, watermelon, grapes; apples, pears and sweet cherries; natural sugars and sweeteners; dried fruit (dates, figs, apricots, mulberries and apples); all carbohydrate-rich foods such as sweet potatoes, squash, grains; most vegetables such as peppers, tomatoes, cucumbers, avocados.

SALTY & UMAMI FOODS
EARTH

Olives, seaweed, mushrooms (especially wild mushrooms), sundried tomatoes, beetroot, celery, celeriac, umeboshi plums, artichoke, chard, parsley, nutritional yeast, salt, tamari, coconut aminos, miso.

DISCOVERING THE NECTAR

When it comes to choosing specific ingredients, whether it is more medicinal and stimulating foods such as coffee, tea, chocolate and sweeteners; regular staples such as vegetables and nuts; or more treasured items such as flower pollen, we encourage you to search your local area to find producers, growers and suppliers who are putting their heart into what they do and care about the intricate web of ecosystems – from bee welfare, to soil health, to the quality of environments – that those ingredients come from. We call this a practice of discovering the nectar. If you choose to drink coffee, enjoy the quest of finding the very best. If you love tomatoes, find ones that taste so good that you can eat them by the handful without having to add any salt. If you appreciate honey, find honey from holistic, artisan beekeepers who keep their bees on wild, biodiverse and organic ecosystems. Yes, the produce might be more expensive, but it will also make you more mindful about consuming these products. Not only is higher-quality produce more satisfying, its greater nutrient density means you will be more fulfilled on a smaller amount. You will also be casting a powerful vote every time you make those choices.

When it comes to mass-produced ingredients, anything from coffee to peanuts and cacao, making a more mindful choice of an artisan, single-origin, wild-crafted ingredient also ensures that it is less likely to be covered in various pathogens. When something is produced with less care, it tends to have a weaker biology and immune system and so is susceptible to all manner of infestation. The more something is grown with awareness and responsiveness, which is how the wilder foods grow, then the more holistically nourishing

it is. On the other hand, when something is grown with an agenda for profit and greed (which is the opposite of how the wilder foods grow) the more it leads to ripples of imbalance and distortions in all the relationships proceeding from it.

Most unpleasant and allergic reactions are due to the compromised biology of ingredients. For example, the aflatoxins on the less cared-for varieties of peanuts, coffee and cacao tend to cause more allergic reactions and other imbalances in our bodies than the more intact genetics of those foods grown in ecologically biodiverse and cared-for environments. The same tendencies are also noticeable in the rise of allergies to the most adulterated and hybridised foods, such as wheat, compared to less processed ancient varieties such as spelt and kamut.

IN THE KITCHEN AND BEYOND

The way to transform what we eat and upgrade our habits has to come from within, guided by the synthesis of the body, mind and soul. It has to feel good to you and go beyond the ever-changeable trends: this way you know that you are on the right track.

We are not suggesting that you omit certain food groups and restrict yourself; we are merely opening more doors to more possibilities, to more variety, and more fun in the kitchen and beyond. All the foods that the garden of earth produces have their part to play in our lives and bodies, each of them containing medicinal elements that may be more or less suitable to our specific situations.

Before we dive into the world of ingredients and recipes let's remember that what works in one direction for us at one point, may not work for us in another direction at another point. Any individual item can be either the appropriate or inappropriate thing for us in each moment, based on quantity, quality and circumstance among many other factors. It is of paramount importance that whatever foods we are making and enjoying, we are observant, inquisitive, intrigued to deepen our awareness and understanding, open to listening to all our feelings and senses, willing to study, investigate and explore all its aspects, and that the final result tastes and feels outrageously delicious and outstandingly nutritious to us. Ultimately, that it truly serves our bodies and our lives.

Some recipes might have ingredients and processes that are unfamiliar to you (see Ingredient guide, page 210 and Equipment, page 208). If that is the case, we are happy! Don't feel pressured into buying a whole cupboardful of new ingredients (unless you are genuinely inspired to); wherever possible, we have provided substitutes and lists of optional ingredients for you to choose from. Instead, take it as an invitation to keep exploring, playing and learning what's possible and available in the plant food kitchen and beyond. Dive in at your own pace, taking your own preferences, location and availability into consideration.

In the same way, try the practices and rituals that resonate with you. Incorporating them into your daily or seasonal routine is one of the key aspects of full-spectrum nourishment, and will, inevitably and over a short period of time, bring more naturalness, balance and thriving to your life. All the rituals and practices we share in this book have been adapted and experienced by us with many positive results; yet they have existed as an intrinsic part of human technology in various shapes and forms since time immemorial. They work regardless of your belief system; they are timeless and by default bring more timelessness into our lives. As a core part of our holistic make-up, they cultivate natural elemental connection; awareness of our own individual compass; and, in the increased

intensity of modern times, create more space for the wisdom of the wild to seep through and permeate our experience.

USING THIS BOOK

The knowledge of this book is arranged following the rhythm and the flow of the Wild Wellbeing Compass (see page 13), with chapters dedicated to each of the four elements (Air, Fire, Water, Earth) and the three realms – up (the cosmos), down, (the earth), and the middle (life), which completes the full circle and signifies the heart of our human existence. Each element also corresponds to one of the four seasons, times of the day, and one of the four compass directions. The book is a dynamic living resource that moves in a cycle, just like the seasons of nature. It doesn't have a beginning or end, and you will find elements of the whole, and the whole of the elements in different aspects of it.

Within each chapter you will find information about the element itself, the season and the time of the day it relates to, guidance on corresponding natural environments and rituals and practices to help you tune in and flow with the rhythm of the wild. The four main chapters, those that tie in to the four elements, have rituals and a selection of our favourite recipes that will guide you day to day, season to season. The final three chapters carry an invitation into a further alchemical adventure of full-spectrum nourishment: wild, wonderful, cosmic and earthy all at the same time.

The seasons and times of the day are never experienced in a vacuum. Everything has a bit of everything else in it. Like a big cosmic soup, the recipes in each chapter will be applicable and usable throughout the whole year, perhaps with a few seasonal adjustments. Take note of the keys next to each recipe; these denote the main seasonality of the dish. We have added notes about seasonal variations where possible but feel free to explore your own.

Keys used throughout the book

As you move through the book you will notice that each recipe has a note to indicate the season, the optimum time of day, and which category of food it falls into. For example:

| All Seasons | All day | Energising |

KNOW

AIR

ENVIRONMENT

Air is the spirit of the East, which can be called upon (by facing this direction) to awaken and activate fresh starts and new beginnings. It is the place of the rising sun, and the time of our birth and earliest childhood. In its essence it has a quality of dryness and carries a bitter flavour spectrum. In our bodies it is represented by our mental activity, the knowledge of ourselves. Early morning is known as the most conducive time for meditation, contemplation and intention-setting as all things begin with a thought in the mind — an idea, a vision, an inspiration. It is associated with planting and sprouting seeds in the springtime. Symbolically, it is represented by our winged and feathered friends, red and orange crystals and the aroma of cedar smoke. It is the waxing moon.

Air is the first element because it is the subtlest. Thus, it makes sense to start the day, cycle or season with inner and outer lightness and gradually utilise more depth of richness according to our requirements — both in our wellbeing practices and in our food. Acknowledge and celebrate the energies of the dawn, the springtime and the air. This is the time when our mind wakes up, our 'daily dawn', so it makes sense to nourish the mind with environments, rituals and foods to prepare us for the day ahead and support our path to more mental balance, clarity and vision. The way we start our day will likely be the way it continues, so creating magnificent morning practices is of the highest good.

RITUALS

RE-WILD THE BREATH

The way we breathe is the way we live. Breath is deeply connected to our minds and our electrical nervous system. It also happens to be the very first nourishment that we receive when we are born, coming even before our mother's milk. Breath helps us think and perceive clearly and connect with our inner guidance.

It is easy to notice that when we are stressed our breath becomes shallow; we pretty much forget to breathe altogether. When we are at ease, our breath is steady and engages the whole abdomen, filling our body with delicious, nourishing oxygen, hydrogen and nitrogen with each inhale. Allowing a few deep breaths to flood through us and wash our cells with oxygen and life force, will bring us in touch with our body and the innate intelligence of our whole being.
Learning to navigate different mental and emotional states with a single breath is easy. Whenever you feel out of balance or in a difficult situation, take a couple of long, calm breaths and picture yourself in a natural environment – perhaps in a forest or in your favourite holiday spot – inhaling the sweetness of fresh air. Make a habit of working with your breath in the morning, and you will have a solid practice to come back to during the day, at moments of stress, anxiety and overwhelm. You will immediately have our own medicine available to you – the conscious use of air and each of those precious deep breaths.

Wild practice: some breathing exercises

ACTIVATING | Make sure you are lying down or sitting comfortably. Breathe so deeply that the strength of the breath gives you a triumphant surge of life force. Breathe with intensity for a couple of minutes, but without it feeling forced. Finish with three regular inhales and exhales. Relax.

CALMING | Try the Kriya Breath: sit in a relaxed posture, scan your body from top to bottom, inviting the muscles of each body part to soften with your gentle attention. Inhale very gradually through the back of your throat, producing a sound of ocean waves, for 10–15 seconds. Exhale gradually for 10–15 seconds. Breathe in inspiration, exhale all that you wish to let go, relax. Finish with three regular inhales and exhales, and a moment of centred meditation to soak in the regenerative benefits of this breath.

PERSONALISE | Use a couple of drops of organic essential oil on your wrists, to guide your inner landscape when working with breath. Try peppermint and rosemary for awareness, focus and activation of the mind; chamomile and lavender for relaxation; frankincense for clearing and purifying any thoughts or emotions that we no longer want to experience; geranium for bringing balance; lemon for uplifting your inner state; and so on. Please note when working with essential oils, always read the user guide and use a carrier oil to apply topically.

THE MEDICINE OF GETTING UP EARLY

Getting up with or even ahead of the sun can be a very powerful tool to help us reconnect with the larger rhythms of the wild. In many traditions, the energy of early mornings is widely considered as the most potent, the most conductive, the most peaceful, the most contemplative time of the day. It can provide us with inner strength, clarity, peace, spaciousness, connection and inner freedom. Waking up early in the morning sends out a very important message: 'Hey, here I am, awake, aware, tuned-in, and ready to take a stand with the first morning light'. We find that being conscious and awake early in the morning gives us the precious time to revel in our own presence. It gives enormous power, strength, clarity, vitality, centredness, and focus that is most appropriate for this time of day.

AWAKENING INTO OUR BODIES

Spend 5–10 minutes simply stretching, doing gentle yoga, walking, taking a refreshing shower or anything that awakens your limbs, re-embodies your senses, shakes off the energy of the night and provides an opportunity to remind yourself how precious your body is. Notice that most of the mammals have a little stretch routine after they awaken. From this place of nourishment, we get more clarity of mind and emotions to raise our internal 'altitude' above the heaviness of the sleep. Most importantly, stretch and awaken your inner and your outer smile.

THE ART OF INTENTION SETTING

Morning is a perfect time to look ahead into our day with a bit of expansiveness, distance and perspective. If we sit very still, our mind still, we can see and feel our day ahead. Being aware of the qualities of this particular day and setting an intention for it is so helpful in establishing a focus of energy to carry with us throughout the day. For example, set an intention to meditate on beauty, strength, focus, equanimity, balance, joy, mastery, inspiration, perseverance, trust – whatever you feel it is you will require during the day. Even better, you can tune in your intention to the cycles of the seasons or the moon. For example, set the intention of new beginnings with the new moon and wrapping up projects with the full moon. Set intention for renewal and regeneration in spring, for manifestation of your projects in autumn and for inner peace and tranquillity in winter. Then you know that your intention is in tune with the bigger rhythm; that you are a part of the vast flow of nature. Feel that state in your body before leaving your house and remember it throughout the day, in the middle of all the action, hustle and bustle. It will hold and support you as an anchor through challenging situations. When we master this moment, we can master the day, the week, the month, the year, the decade, and eventually, the lifetime.

BREAK THE FAST

We break the fast each morning as we wake up. Some say that every fool knows how to fast, but only a master knows how to break the fast. Take a moment to give thanks before eating the first food of the day. Extend this practice to all your meals and reap the benefits of more mindfulness, better digestion and a more harmonious, intuitive relationship with food. Food is a nourishment for body, mind and spirit so bringing ourselves to the point of presence and gratitude at the beginning a meal is the most important practice to nourish ourselves from the present moment. It gradually develops our taste buds and intuition of what our bodies require at any given time, as it makes sure we are not running on autopilot. It is a collective practice we've been doing since day one during team breakfast at Wild Food Café and it works wonders.

You may have experienced the effects of being doubled over with indigestion from eating while in a bad mood. When we eat while feeling stressed or anxious, these emotions become solidified, exaggerated and trapped in our system. Focus on the experience of dining, rather than multitasking or looking at your devices while you eat. Make it your time, your wellbeing ritual, your meditation and your altar. In many ways it doesn't matter what's on your plate: cherish it. Remember all the people, plants, animals and ecosystems that contributed to the meal in front of you. It is a miracle. Enjoying every meal with gratitude will make you feel amazing inside and out. Your body and your digestion will thank you for it and you will naturally feel better and happier.

EDIBLES

The morning – and correspondingly the spring – is a natural time for gentle detoxification: it is a time of breaking the fast, so it requires an insightful intention. In the morning we've woken up our bodies which have been regenerating and cleansing. We start with water, move on to a herbal tea, then into other forms of liquid nourishment, such as juices, thicker smoothies and bowls, displaying a scale from subtle to dense in our morning meal. The top priority for our morning drink is that it is yummy and wholesomely satisfying with a slow release of energy that will fuel us for a good few hours. In summer we choose lighter and fruitier smoothies (see Pink Heart Medicine pages 39-40, and Wild Lemonade page 34); in winter we go for richer, denser, warmer drinks (see Wild Whip page 49, Divine Pine page 52 and Medicinal Mushroom Latte page 53). We feel and taste continuously and notice how our body, thoughts and emotions respond. We use these tools to guide our choices. All of this happens before we even proceed to solid food.

WILD WISDOM

Upon waking up, start with a glass of room temperature or warm water as a blank canvas for your body and for your day. Start with plain or personalised flavoured water, then move on to herbal tea (see page 202).

FORGOTTEN ECSTASY

Since the day we opened the Wild Food Café, we have heard so many stories of guests travelling from far and wide – sometimes coming straight from the airport – to enjoy a glass of Forgotten Ecstasy. It is the best cacao smoothie of all time.

- 170g (6oz) cacao paste
- 500ml (18fl oz/2 cups) water at room temperature (plus extra if needed)
- 200g (7oz/1⅛ cups) chopped dates
- 1 tbsp maple syrup
- 50g (1¾oz/generous ½ cup) coconut meat
- 1 tbsp maca
- 1 tbsp he-shou-wu (optional)
- pinch of salt
- 200ml (7fl oz/generous ¾ cup) coconut water

TO SERVE
- Chocolate Sauce (see below)

CHOCOLATE SAUCE
(Makes 500ml/18fl oz/ 2 cups)
- 175g (6oz/1½ cups) cacao powder
- 1½ tbsp maple syrup
- pinch of salt

● **Serves 2–4**

Place the roughly chopped cacao paste and water in a high-speed blender, blending fully until a smooth consistency with no grainy texture. Be careful not to over-blend the mixture. Add the dates, maple syrup and coconut meat and blend until smooth. Add the maca, he-shou-wu (if using), salt and coconut water followed by up to 500ml (18fl oz/2 cups) of water to make it up to 2 litres (3½ pints/8 cups), and blend until smooth.

To make the chocolate sauce, place all the ingredients in a high-speed blender and blend until combined, alternatively whisk in a mixing bowl. Transfer to a squeezy bottle. This will keep in the fridge for up to a week.

To serve, line a glass with some of the Chocolate Sauce and fill with the smoothie mix. Top with more Chocolate Sauce to decorate.

GOGENIUS ELIXIR

This elixir provides a full spectrum of nourishment for a healthy genius mind. The vivid colour keeps our mind happy, while the walnuts, with their brain-like appearance, contain omega oils, which are the perfect replacement for fish oils and support the brain in its optimum functioning.

- 60g (2oz/½ cup) dried goji berries
- 800ml (28fl oz/ 3⅓ cups) water
- 140g (5oz/1½ cups) redcurrants

- 40g (1½oz/⅓ cup) dried walnuts
- 100g (3½oz) ice cubes
- pinch of salt
- 1 tbsp xylitol (or sweetener of your choice)
- 1–10 drops sea buckthorn oil (optional)

- ½ tsp schisandra berry (optional)
- 1 capsule golden algae oil (optional)
- 1 tbsp sunflower lecithin (optional)

● **Serves 2–4**

Soak the goji berries in the measured water for around 1 hour. Blend the goji berries with their soaking water until smooth. Add the redcurrants and walnuts to the blender and blend again. Finally add the ice, salt, xylitol and also the sea buckthorn oil, schisandra, golden algae oil and sunflower lecithin, if using – and blend until smooth.

WILD WISDOM

Feel free to replace the redcurrants with fresh or frozen sea buckthorn, raspberries, cherries or other sour red berries of your choice.

COCONUT DURIAN CACAO SMOOTHIE

Like other fine things in life (which we call 'nectar foods') – such as good wine, coffee, chocolate, honey, artichokes and olives – consuming durian is an acquired taste experience. If there is an occasion in your life that requires a daring, adventurous, sexy, decadent, lush and heart-opening potion – this is it. This is not an everyday smoothie, but is a fabulous addition to a special occasion.

- 2 young Thai coconuts
- 5 small dates or 1 tbsp wildcrafted honey
- 500g (1lb 2oz) frozen durian, without pits
- ½ vanilla pod, split and scraped, or 1 tsp vanilla essence
- pinch of salt
- 1 tsp chaga powder or extract (optional)
- ½ cup ice cubes
- 30g (1¼oz/¼ cup) cacao nibs

Serves 2–4

Carefully open both coconuts, pour the coconut water into a container, then scoop out the flesh with a spoon.

Place the coconut flesh in a high-speed blender, add the dates if you are using them, and pour just enough coconut water on top to cover the coconut flesh. Blend until you get a smooth coconut cream.

Remove the plastic wrapper from the frozen durian pods (if present) under a stream of warm water and cut the durian into small slices with a sturdy knife or cleaver.

Add the durian, remaining coconut water, honey (if you haven't used dates), vanilla, salt and chaga powder, if using, to the blender. Blend again until smooth.

If the smoothie consistency is too thick, add some ice cubes at this stage to reach optimum consistency and blend again. Finally, add the cacao nibs and whiz for just a second to keep a slight chocolate chip crunch. Serve.

WILD LEMONADE

The beauty of this recipe is in using the whole lemon. By choosing organic, unwaxed lemons (or limes) we can blend the whole fruit and benefit from using the rind, pith and seeds. It is a great antiviral and antifungal drink. High in bioflavonoids, there are two or three times more vitamin C in the pith than in the pulp. There is fresh essential oil in the rind, and it is flavoursome and aromatic. Unlike many lemonades you've come across, this one is a nutritional powerhouse and is an excellent post-workout drink.

- 3 organic, unwaxed lemons (or limes)
- 3 ripe pears or apples
- 5cm (2-inch) piece of fresh turmeric
- 2.5cm (1-inch) piece of fresh root ginger
- 1 tsp ground Sichuan pepper
- ½ tsp ground cinnamon
- 1 tbsp coconut oil
- 1 tbsp hemp seeds or olive oil
- pinch of salt
- 1 tbsp pine pollen
- 500ml (18fl oz/2 cups) water
- 3 tbsp xylitol
- 10 drops liquid stevia
- 6–7 ice cubes
- 240ml (8fl oz/1 cup) kombucha (optional)

● **Serves 2–4**

Start by scrubbing the lemons or limes and chopping them into quarters. Add them to a high-speed blender and blend with the rest of the ingredients except the ice cubes and kombucha, until smooth. Sweeten further if necessary to taste. Add enough ice to make it up to 1 litre (1¾ pints/4 cups) and blend again.

The lemonade without the kombucha is smooth and creamy. If you prefer a thinner consistency resembling a traditional lemonade, fill half a glass with the lemonade and fill the rest with kombucha of your choice.

WILD WISDOM

We use Sichuan pepper due to its tingly, cooling sensation that goes so well with lemonade. Feel free to replace with freshly ground black pepper.

MELONADE

A wonderful summer's drink, great to refresh and cool you down.

- 1 small melon
  (approximately 1.5kg/
  3lb 5oz)
- 2 limes or lemons
- 250ml (8½fl oz/1 cup) water

- 300g (10½oz) ice cubes
- 100g (3½oz/1½ cups) kale
- 50g (1¾oz/1 cup) parsley,
  coriander or rocket
- 25g (1oz/1 cup) mint

- 1½ tbsp coconut oil
- 1 tbsp xylitol or sweetener
  of choice
- 240ml (8fl oz/1 cup)
  coconut water

● **Serves 2–4**

Peel the melon with a vegetable peeler. Chop the limes or lemons into quarters, leaving the skin on. Add the flesh and seeds of the melon and the chopped limes or lemons to a high-speed blender, blending with the measured water and 150g (5½oz) of the ice cubes.

Once a smooth milk is achieved, add all the greens and the rest of the ice and blend until smooth. Strain though a nut milk bag or a sieve if it is not fine enough (it might be the case if you don't have a high-speed blender). Add the remaining ingredients and blend again.

WILD WISDOM

The first benefit of this recipe is that it introduces a new way to eat a melon, taking the thinnest, driest piece of rind off using a peeler, and using every other part of the melon. If you have a strong-enough blender, pulverize the seeds to make a melon-seed milk first. These are the freshest seeds you can get.

PINK HEART MEDICINE I

This smoothie is filling, opulent and grounding. It is designed to have the benefits of a green juice due to its high mineral content, while retaining the wonderful pink colour of the watermelon and cherries.

- 5cm (2-inch) piece of fresh root ginger or 2 tsp ground ginger
- 800g (1lb 12oz) watermelon
- 200g (7oz/1½ cups) pitted cherries (or raspberries)

- 100g (3½oz/⅔ cup) frozen sour cherries
- 40g (1½oz/¼ cup) shelled hemp seeds
- 2 tbsp lucuma powder

- pinch of salt
- 1–2 tsp cacao butter, melted (optional)
- 1 tbsp organic liquid trace minerals (optional)

Serves 2–4

Start by juicing the ginger, then set aside.

Add the watermelon and cherries or raspberries to a high-speed blender and blend until smooth. Then add the frozen sour cherries and the hemp seeds and blend again until smooth. Add the ginger juice, lucuma powder and salt, cacao butter and organic liquid trace minerals, if using, and give it a final blend.

WILD WISDOM

If you don't have a juicer or prefer not to juice the ginger separately, feel free to use 2 tsp of ground ginger instead of the fresh root ginger.

PINK HEART MEDICINE II

Although there is currently some discussion about whether you should combine melons or watermelons with other foods, we have found that in a smoothie form it is a nice occasional treat and works perfectly well for our digestive systems.

- 5cm (2-inch) piece of fresh root ginger or 2 tsp ground ginger
- 1.3kg (3lb) watermelon
- 150g (5½oz/1 cup) pitted cherries (or raspberries)

- 60g (2oz/⅓ cup) frozen sour cherries
- 300g (10½oz/3¾ cups) coconut meat

- 50ml (2fl oz/¼ cup) coconut milk
- juice of ½ lime
- 6 small ice cubes
- pinch of salt

● **Serves 2–4**

Start by juicing the ginger, then set aside.

Add the watermelon and cherries or raspberries to a high-speed blender and blend until smooth. Add the frozen sour cherries and blend again. Add the coconut meat and coconut milk and blend until smooth. Add the ginger juice, lime juice, ice cubes and salt and give it a final blend.

WILD MARY

Juices don't always have to be sweet. They can be satisfyingly rich in deep umami and savoury flavours and start blurring the lines within the realm of raw soups. This is our favourite drink for brunch or a midday pick-me-up.

- 600ml (1 pint/2½ cups) tomato juice
- 2 tsp ginger juice
- 2 tsp lemon juice
- 2 tsp Worcestershire Sauce (see page 43)
- 2 tsp Chilli Sauce (see page 43)
- 4 ice cubes
- pinch of salt

TO DECORATE
- maple syrup
- activated charcoal
- stick of celery
- twist of freshly ground black pepper

Decorate a juice glass by dipping the rim into maple syrup and then pressing it into activated charcoal mixed with a little salt.

Pour all the smoothie ingredients straight into a jug, add ice cubes and a pinch of salt and serve. Garnish individual glasses with a celery stick and a twist of freshly ground black pepper.

● Serves 2–4

WILD WISDOM

This drink is an excellent and resourceful use of fresh tomato juice left over from making gazpacho, bruschetta or other tomato-rich recipes.

With extra unpasteurised miso added you can lengthen the shelf life of the sauces.

CONTINUED OVERLEAF

WILD MARY CONTINUED

WORCESTERSHIRE SAUCE
(Makes 500ml/18fl oz/2 cups)
– 30ml (1fl oz/⅛ cup) apple cider vinegar
– 100g (3½oz/generous ½ cup) dates or dried figs
– 30ml (1fl oz/⅛ cup) tamari or coconut aminos
– 65ml (2½fl oz/¼ cup) water

– 1 tbsp miso paste
– 2 tbsp lemon juice
– 1 tbsp tamarind fruit pulp or paste
– 2 tsp ginger juice
– 5½ tsp salt
– 4 peppercorns
– 1 tsp onion powder
– 1 tsp garlic powder
– ¼ tsp cayenne pepper

– ½ tsp ground cinnamon

CHILLI SAUCE
(Makes 250ml/8½fl oz/1 cup)
– 50g (1¾oz) fresh chillies
– 125ml (4fl oz/½ cup) apple cider vinegar
– 80ml (3fl oz/⅓ cup) olive oil
– pinch of salt

WORCESTERSHIRE SAUCE
Blend all the ingredients in a high-speed blender on high until smooth. Strain and taste for consistency – you want a gently spiced, sour flavour. This will keep in the fridge for up to a week.

CHILLI SAUCE
Roughly chop the chillies into fine pieces. Add all the ingredients to a high-speed blender and blend together until smooth. This will keep in the fridge for up to 2 weeks.

PRINCE OF PERSIA

Pomegranate is one of the most unique and ancient of winter fruits, with many ways to enjoy it. Although we highly recommend juicing it in a masticating juicer or in a manual orange press for its ruby red juice, this version utilises both the juice and the wonderful creamy milk from the seed within the kernel, giving us a naturally pink-coloured sweet milk complemented by the delicate rose water.

- 400g (14oz) pomegranate seeds
- 400g (14oz) frozen pomegranate seeds
- pinch of salt
- 20g (¾oz) soaked dulse, drained
- a few drops of rose water (to taste)
- 6–10 drops liquid stevia (according to taste and sweetness of the pomegranate)
- 1 tbsp of rose petals (optional)

● Serves 2–4

Add the fresh and frozen pomegranate seeds to a high-speed blender and blend until smooth. Add the salt and strain through a chinois or muslin. Add the soaked dulse, rose water and stevia to the strained pomegranate milk and blend lightly again. Pour into glasses and decorate with the rose petals if you wish.

WILD WISDOM

Prepare the frozen pomegranate seeds in advance. The pith inside the pomegranate (the white bits) is a very strong medicine and while very bitter, contains more antioxidants than the actual juice. If you are feeling adventurous, allow a few small bits of pith to make it into your blender.

PLANET OF THE GRAPES

We love blending grapes to extract the medicinal goodness from the seeds and skin. Grape seeds and skins contain resveratrol as well as other potent antioxidants known for their youthening and protective effects; as well as vitamin E, which is so soothing for our skin. Rather than buying an expensive separate grape seed extract, go wild and enjoy this elixir every autumn, when the best grapes come into season.

- 400g (14oz) fresh muscat grapes
- 400g (14oz) frozen muscat grapes

- 4½ tsp organic liquid trace minerals
- 1 tsp rhodiola rosea (optional)

- 3½ tsp schisandra (optional)

Serves 2–4

Add the fresh and frozen grapes and the organic liquid trace minerals to a high-speed blender and blend for around 2 minutes until all the ingredients combine. Pour the mixture through a chinois or muslin and add a mixture of rhodiola and schisandra for an extra nutrition boost if you wish. Serve.

WILD WISDOM

It is the epitome of 'un-wildness' to consume seedless fruit: it is not something one comes across in nature! The grapes used in this drink should always be organic grapes with seeds, as they come with so many benefits. To make a smoother experience of eating crunchy grape seeds and their skin, simply juice and/ or blend the whole grape and then strain it through a chinois or muslin. You can use the leftover pulp in a sweet cracker or cookie recipe or as a full body exfoliant.

WILD WHIP

The wild whip is a combination of an intense, tangy vitamin C hit and the spiciness of ginger, which is wonderfully complementary. It is such a mood-boosting drink – just the colours of it will make you happy. There is two to three times more vitamin C in the pith of citrus fruit, as well as bioflavonoids, which helps the body to absorb vitamins.

- 400ml sea buckthorn juice
- 4 medium or 6 small whole clementines, oranges or blood oranges
- 1 red pepper
- 4 tbsp goji berries
- 2 tbsp Inca berries
- 2 tbsp maple syrup or 6–8 dates
- 50ml ginger juice

● **Serves 2–4**

In a blender jug, pour the sea buckthorn juice, clementines or citrus of choice, red pepper, goji berries, Inca berries, maple syrup and ginger juice into a high-speed blender and blend twice. Strain through a chinois or muslin.

WILD WISDOM

When making this drink in spring/summer we would recommend usinge redcurrants and fresh berries instead of the dry berries, and omitting the ginger.

VIBRANT GREEN

If we had to pick one juice or smoothie to have every day, this would be it. We always change it up with the season, however, what doesn't change is the lush, fresh green plants that go in it and nourish our cells with vibrant plant chlorophyll and an abundance of alkalising trace minerals. So much plant goodness in one glass (or jug). It is up to you as an individual to find an ever-dynamic balance between being able to enjoy as much of the stronger-flavoured bitter, sour, medicinal greens as possible in a ratio with fruits and vegetables.

GREEN BASE
(makes 500ml/18fl oz/2 cups)
- 75g (2¾oz/1 cup) kale
- 5g (⅛oz) samphire

- 5g (⅛oz) nettle
- 50g (1¾oz/1½ cups) watercress
- 50g (1¾oz/2 cups) basil

- 100ml (3½fl oz/scant ½ cup) lemon juice
- Up to 500ml (18fl oz/ 2 cups) of water

You can replace the samphire and nettle with any of the following: dandelion, cleavers, plantain leaf, thistle, lamb's quarter, purslane, mustard leaf, clover, chickweed, hemp leaf, amaranth leaf or any of the cultivated greens listed below.

You can replace the kale, watercress or basil with: parsley, coriander, rocket, spinach, mint or sorrel.

● **Serves 2–4**

METHOD I WITH THE GREEN BASE:
Typically, we make a juice and blend in the greens in an acid-rich juice base (such as lemon) that immediately preserves it. If you don't have a green juicer, this option is especially convenient.

To make the base, put half the greens and all the lemon juice in a high-speed blender along with just enough water to ensure blending and blend well. Add the remaining greens. Blend on high until smooth, ensuring the mix doesn't overheat. Add more water as needed – up to approximately 500ml (18fl oz/2 cups). Depending on the strength of your blender and the result you

JUICE
- 10–12 sticks of celery
- 1 long cucumber
- 5–6 apples
- 1.25cm (½-inch) piece of fresh root ginger
- 2 tsp lemon juice
- 200ml (7fl oz/generous ¾ cup) Green Base (see opposite)
- 1 tsp spirulina

are looking for, it may require straining through a chinois or nut milk bag. This base will keep in the fridge for up to 3 days and can be frozen into ice cubes.

To make the juice, juice the celery, cucumber, apples and ginger. Blend the measured Green Base with all the juice and the spirulina and serve.

METHOD II:
If you have a masticating green juicer, simply put all the vegetables and herbs through the juicer, then blend in the spirulina and 100ml (3½fl oz/scant ½ cup) of lemon juice.

DIVINE PINE

This is a wonderful mix of many aspects of the pine tree. Embodying the spirit of the Christmas tree and plant-based Christmas alchemy, it transports us to the middle of a wintry forest and is an ode to the forest and pine family in particular. Pine trees have impressive lifespans, stretching up to 1,000 years, while the most ancient is known to be over 4,500 years old. Pine gives a wonderfully refreshing fragrance, so many antiseptic products are infused with essence of pine.

- 8 large kale leaves
- 10 tsp finely chopped Douglas fir, Scots pine and spruce
- 1 tsp lemon juice
- 1 tsp salt
- 8 tbsp pine nuts
- 8 tsp pine pollen (optional)
- 10 tsp spirulina
- 1 tsp ginger juice
- zest of 1 lemon
- 10 tsp ground cinnamon
- 300ml (10fl oz/1¼ cups) apple juice, per glass

● **Serves 2–4**

To make a base, add the kale, Douglas fir, Scots pine and spruce, lemon juice and salt with as little water as possible to a high-speed blender and blend until smooth.

Pass through a chinois or muslin and add the pine nuts, pine pollen, if using, spirulina, ginger juice, lemon zest and cinnamon and blend until smooth. Add the apple juice and mix with the green base then serve.

WILD WISDOM

The needle of the pine is very rich in vitamin C and can be used in fresh herbal teas and ritual bath infusions, or blended into smoothies. You can also add a tea of pine bark and pine cone. When working with new and unusual wild foods you should use discretion and research them and add them slowly, checking which are appropriate in conditions such as pregnancy and breastfeeding.

MEDICINAL MUSHROOM LATTE

We love these nourishing, medicinal mushrooms in a drink form, and they don't taste anything like regular mushrooms! In particular, the chaga mushroom has a wonderful vanilla flavour. The other medicinal mushrooms have rich, earthy, nutty, slightly bitter and coffee-like flavours and go really well with frothy nut milks.

- 200ml (7fl oz/generous ¾ cup) almond milk
- 2 tsp ground cinnamon, plus extra to sprinkle
- 2 tsp mushroom complex powder
- 2 tsp coconut oil
- pinch of salt
- 2 tsp maple syrup
- ¼ tsp dandelion root powder (optional)
- ¼ tsp burdock root powder (optional)
- 1 tsp sunflower lecithin (optional)
- 300ml (10fl oz/1¼ cups) hot water

TO GARNISH
- Caramel Sauce (see below)
- Ground cinnamon, to sprinkle

CARAMEL SAUCE
(Makes 250ml/8½fl oz/ 1 cup)
- 150g (5½oz/1 cup) dates
- 250ml (8½fl oz/ 1 cup) water

Add the almond milk to a high-speed blender along with the cinnamon, mushroom complex powder, coconut oil, salt and maple syrup as well as the dandelion root powder, burdock root powder and sunflower lecithin, if using. Add the hot water and blend well.

To make the caramel sauce, blend the dates and water until smooth.

Line a glass or mug with the Caramel Sauce then pour in the frothy mushroom latte mix, sprinkle with cinnamon to decorate.

● **Serves 2**

53

COCONUT YOGHURT WITH HOLY GRANOLA

Whenever we fancy a luxurious breakfast – especially at our retreats and residential programmes – we go for our signature coconut yoghurt with granola. It works every time.

COCONUT YOGHURT
- 160g (5¾oz/2 cups) fresh coconut meat
- 240ml (8fl oz/1 cup) coconut water
- 2 tsp probiotic powder
- 3 tbsp maple syrup
- 2 tbsp lemon juice

TO SERVE
- A selection of fresh or dried seasonal berries of your choice

● Serves 2–4

Make the yoghurt and granola at least a day in advance. Blend the coconut meat and coconut water in a high-speed blender until you get a very smooth texture. Transfer to a bowl and mix in the probiotic powder. Cover the bowl and leave at room temperature for 24 hours. The next day, add maple syrup and lemon juice to taste (depending on how sour you want it to be) then refrigerate.

To make the granola, mix all the ingredients in a bowl and stir until well combined. Place the mixture gently onto dehydrator sheets without pressing or squeezing it. Dehydrate at 45°C/113°F overnight. The next morning, flip the granola and put it back in for another 6 hours or until dry and crunchy. If using fan-assisted oven, use the lowest temp setting until dry and crunchy.

Serve the yoghurt and granola with a selection of fresh berries or seasonal fruit.

WILD WISDOM

Make a batch of coconut yoghurt and use it in both sweet and savoury dishes. This will keep in the fridge for up to a week.

GRANOLA

- 25g (1oz) mixed puffs
  (quinoa, amaranth or rice)
- 25g (1oz/3½ tbsp)
  pumpkin seeds
- 50g (1¾oz/⅓ cup)
  sunflower seeds
- 30g (1¼oz/⅓ cup)
  coconut flakes
- 50g (1¾oz/½ cup) pecans
- 2½ tbsp cacao nibs
- 4 tbsp cacao powder
- 45g (1½oz/½ cup)
  flaked almonds
- ½ tbsp ground cinnamon
- ½ tbsp mesquite
- ½ tbsp maca
- 140g (5oz/scant ½ cup)
  maple syrup
- 1 tbsp vanilla extract
- 30g (1¼oz/¼ cup)
  coconut sugar
- 1½ tbsp chopped walnuts
- ½ tbsp orange zest
- 120ml (4fl oz/½ cup)
  orange juice
- 80g (3oz/½ cup) buckwheat

MILLET WHITE MISO PORRIDGE

Aiste: 'Be it millet, oat or amaranth, I am a lover of savoury porridges, and I trust you will fall in love with this one, too. Even though I am up for eating porridge at any time of the day, I am a believer that mornings shouldn't be started with a sweet breakfast. Anything savoury and umami tastes so good in the morning and a little bit of chilli gives a kick for extra-cold mornings.'

- 120g (4oz) cooked millet
- 200ml (7fl oz/generous ¾ cup) coconut milk
- 1 tomato, finely chopped
- 2 handfuls of baby spinach or sorrel
- 1 tbsp white miso
- 5mm (¼-inch) fresh chilli, finely chopped (optional)

Serves 2–4

Millet takes a while to cook, so prepare by cooking a big batch of millet the day before, cool down and store in the fridge for up to 3 days.

For the porridge, start by reheating the millet and coconut milk in a medium-sized saucepan over a medium heat. Stir continuously until the millet is reheated. Add extra water if needed. Turn the heat down to low, add the chopped tomato, spinach or sorrel and white miso and stir well. Finally stir in the chopped chilli, if using. Serve right away.

WILD WISDOM

Try this recipe using different porridge bases including teff flakes, amaranth, quinoa or oat — it is gorgeous!

GLOW

FIRE

ENVIRONMENT

The direction of the South represents the fire within as well as the tribal campfire. Fire sits at the very heart – the centre – of all human experience. Since time immemorial, we have gathered around fires for countless reasons: nourishment, warmth, healing, family, community, celebration and all of life's activities. It carries a naturally mystical, transformative, spiritual quality that mesmerises, nourishes and centres us. Fire represents the height of summer, blossoming and expansion of all kinds, the midday sun, our luminous, inspirationally bright nature. It is the fire of intuition and the mysterious gut feeling that guides us. Symbolically it is represented by heart-centred crystals such as rose quartz, ruby and tiger's eye; by warm-blooded noble pack animals, such as wolves and wild cats. It is associated with the refreshing, uplifting smoke of frankincense or copal resin. Fire is dry in its essence and carries a sour and spicy flavour spectrum. It is represented by the full moon.

A healthy clean heart doesn't just mean our ability to have a functioning body; having healthy fire in our hearts means we can thrive within the context of our lives and the bigger, interconnected whole of society and ecosystem. From a happy heart to a healthy gut, we are the ones that kindle the inner glow of our being. The ability to be skilful fire-keepers corresponds to the clarity of inner connection between our heart, mind and breath. Fire symbolises the enthusiasm to be ourselves, sharing our glow, taking initiative and inspired action.

RITUALS

CONNECTION WITH FIRE

Most of us have adopted the habit of waking up and going to sleep staring at digital screens. Let us remember that all of the technology of our society, from the most sophisticated microchips to combustion engines, to the stainless-steel knives we use in our kitchens, are products of the alchemically transformational powers of fire: their bare components forged in its furnaces. The screens we stare at are merely echoes of the original qualities of a natural fire.

As wonderful as this technology is, it is only as good as our mastery of it. If we are slaves to our technology, then both it and we become relatively useless. Instead of staring at a blue screen, make it a practice to start and finish the day with candlelight, even for just five minutes a day. Sit and watch the fire dance. Notice its flickering and pulsation. Hold your hand on your heart or pulse and tune in to its rhythm; feel your centre. You will feel more in tune with the natural rhythms of sleep and wakefulness, rest better and wake up easier; your internal states will become more balanced. Your eyes will thank you for it. Just remember to respect the fire by never leaving it unattended.

Fire also purifies and sanitises. The Mayan elder Tata Pedro, who conducts fire ceremonies globally, says, 'Fire is the only element humanity has not and cannot pollute'. Connecting daily to a natural fire reconnects us to that intrinsic purity of fire of our heart and soul.

CONNECTION TO THE SUN

The most practical thing you can do each day is to say hi to the sun.

TAINO ELDER MAESTRO
MANUEL RUFINO

Making a commitment to say good morning or good evening to the sun on a regular basis brings immeasurable happiness and gratitude for being alive, uplifts our mood, tops us up with some vitamin D and is invigorating for our mental and emotional health. While greeting the sun is a beautiful practice in its own right, we can extend it further by mindfully practising sun gazing. Although staring directly at the full sun can be dangerous, it is safe to gaze at the sun with our eyelids semi-closed within the first hour of sunrise and the last hour of sunset, when the UV index is minimal (below two). This should be natural, comfortable and not forced. Starting the practice with 15 seconds and increasing it by 15 seconds each proceeding time. Use this practice to recharge your inner fire, rest your eyes and your mind and reconnect with the wild cosmos. You should feel like your brain is recharging directly from the central life source of our solar system.

I feel the fire burning
in my heart
You cannot make me doubt
it in my heart
I feel the fire burning,
I feel the fire burning,
I feel the fire burning
in my heart.

TRADITIONAL FIRE SONG

⚛ Wild practice: sun gazing

Stand barefoot on the earth, without any form of glasses or contact lenses. If it feels natural to squint gently then do so, looking through your eyelashes, otherwise gaze around the general area of the sun, rather than directly at it. Focus your mind with clear intention. The benefits of practising this properly can include improved vision, more positive emotions and attitude, combined with fewer stressful emotions, more energy and the feeling of being well nourished.

MIDDAY RECHARGE

Set your alarm for or around midday each day, when the sun is at its highest. That's when we tend to be at the peak of our activity. Notice where you are at, and what activities you are (and have been) in the middle of. Make an effort to pause, take a few moments to centre into your heart, remind yourself of the directions. Take in as brief or long a moment as you can offer. Feel the sun pouring into and regenerating your being, even when it is cloudy. You will continue your day with renewed awareness and centredness. Follow this with 250–500ml of water or 250–500ml of Invincibilitea (see page 202), then wait 15 minutes before eating. You are guaranteed to make better lunch choices, leaving you feeling more uplifted and vibrant. The cumulative effects of a practice like this are astounding.

EXPOSURE TO HOT AND COLD ENVIRONMENTS

A great way to rebalance our inner fire is to expose ourselves to the natural temperature contrast of hot and cold. In many traditional cultures around the world there is the practice of some sort of sauna contrasted with a cold river, sea, lake or snow. The more versatile we are in adapting to the temperature scale, the more versatile we will be at mastering our mental states and handling our emotions – and consequently our actions. Taking ourselves out of artificially regulated temperature environments is a great medicine whenever we feel that the fire in our bodies has been dimmed or unbalanced. It is especially useful whenever you feel that your blood circulation is low and your feet and hands are always cold. Opening up and exposing ourselves to the full-spectrum playing field of the temperature range reminds us of our most primal adaptivity. Once experienced, we can take that adaptivity with us into our everyday lives.

⚛ Wild practice: hot and cold showers

Take alternating hot and cold showers daily, each lasting one minute. Do as many cycles as possible according to your schedule, especially when you have emotional difficulties or stressful situations. Do your best to finish on a cold setting. Your mind, your nervous system, your skin and your whole being will thank you for it. It is immensely rejuvenating and cleansing as it involves our largest organ (our skin) in a process of feeding and elimination. If you can and have access, make time for wild swimming and saunas all year round.

EDIBLES

In the height of midday activity and, correspondingly, in the height of summer, we are naturally inclined to eat lightly so that whatever we eat doesn't make us feel hotter, heavy, sleepy or put additional strain on our digestive system. When the abundance of fresh vegetables and fruits is at its peak, there is an irresistible pleasure in biting into a huge juicy heirloom tomato, experiencing the crunch of whole cucumber, devouring a punnet of berries or enjoying a big, fresh, crispy salad for lunch. Peeling an avocado by hand, sprinkling it with a little seasoning and eating it right out of your hands is easy, fun, natural and nourishing for your whole self.

The fire in summer and at midday is at its peak and doesn't need more fire thrown on it. It's best to avoid heavily cooked, processed or spicy foods and heavier ingredients such as nuts, seeds and cultured foods, especially if you are already more of a fiery type person. Keep it light, delicious, nutritious, simple and colourful. We naturally gravitate towards raw-centric meals: soups, gazpachos, smoothies (not ice-cold), salads and easy-going snacks, especially for spring and summer lunches.

Hari hachi bu is a famous Japanese discipline of not eating past the feeling of being 80 per cent full. It is a method that ensures that we don't smother the fire in our gut in the busiest part of our day. It doesn't matter how nutritious food is, if we eat too much of it, it spoils our digestion, making us feel bloated, lethargic and unable to concentrate. That's why at lunchtime (as well as in summer in general) we err towards lighter, fresher, easier - to - digest options such as broths, soups or salads.

When, where and how to use fire is a great art that requires continuous personal exploration. Fire – or heat – can destroy and alter the most delicate nutrients and their flavours, but used wisely it can help make edible and enjoyable a great many things. In a recipe, whether it is a soup or a smoothie, the temperature used will greatly affect the flavour sensation. We are also very mindful about boiling things too fiercely, especially when delicate ingredients are involved, keeping the temperature at 60–70°C is often more beneficial to both nutrients and flavours. Take the same recipe and serve it at two different temperatures and you will have greatly varying experiences. When the same five ingredients of a smoothie or a soup are combined in a warmer temperature, there is a wider range of more pronounced separate distinct flavours – the flavours are 'loose' and relaxed. Cool that recipe down, and those flavours will crystallise into a tighter flavour formation profile that is often experienced as milder on our taste buds.

The foods that exaggerate fire are most of the sour foods and the spicy foods – the sorts of food that make us glow (sour), or even give us blushed cheeks (spicy). All cultured foods and probiotics fall into this category and they are intrinsically beautifying, driving more blood around our bodies. Almost any fresh wholefood in a balanced form will work as a natural mood lifter too: the natural elemental quality of the fire.

WATERMELON GAZPACHO

You might have tasted this gazpacho at the Wild Food Café in the summer when it was a staple during long and busy sun-drenched days. It is so good, light and refreshing, we could literally eat multiple bowls of it in one go (and we often do!). It is also super simple to make. Raw food at its best.

- 515g (1lb 2oz) watermelon
- 2 tsp ginger juice
- 100g (3½oz) cucumber
- 3g (⅛oz) chilli
- 100g (3½oz) tomatoes
- 20g (¾oz) spring onions, finely chopped
- 1 tbsp chopped coriander, plus extra to garnish
- juice of 1 lime

Serves 2–4

Blend 340g (12oz) of the watermelon with the ginger juice in a high-speed blender until smooth.

Finely dice the remaining watermelon and the cucumber. Deseed the chilli and tomatoes and dice very finely. Mix the blended watermelon with the rest of the ingredients and chill for 2 hours in the fridge before serving. Add a few coriander leaves on top of each bowl when serving.

BORSCHT

Beetroot and dill is a duo made in heaven (especially for Aiste) – if you are a fan of one, you are bound to love the other. This soup always returns to our kitchen and the Wild Food Café in summer and autumn and can easily be transformed into a hot soup as well, depending on the weather. Any time you are in need of some serious edible colour therapy in your life, this soup is a go-to.

- 250g (9oz) beetroot
- 150g (5½oz) purple carrots
- 150g (5½oz) cauliflower
- 1 small apple
- 100g (3½oz) celery (the least-green part of it – preferably the bottom)

- 40g (1½oz) red onion
- 1 clove of garlic
- 1 lemon
- 500ml (18fl oz/2 cups) water
- 1 tsp salt
- 70g (2½oz/¼ cup) coconut cream

- 1 gherkin
- 4 tbsp tamari
- 250g (9oz) ice cubes (in summer)

TO SERVE
- Sour Cream (see page 127)
- sprigs of dill

Blend all the soup ingredients in a high-speed blender until smooth. Serve with a swirl of sour cream and sprigs of dill. Serve at room temperature or warmed.

● Serves 4–6

KIMCHEE SOUP

Kimchee soup, with its infinite variations, is one of Joel's favourite recipes and was one of the first menu items ever in his pop-up raw restaurant and festival stall. This soup is the most perfect medicine if you feel like your digestion is a little stagnant, or whenever you feel under the weather. Be mindful, though, it is super-heating, so if you feel like you already have fire in your system, consume mindfully and avoid eating this during the hottest of summer days.

- 4 tbsp dried goji berries
- 225g (8oz) kimchee (see page 124)

- 2 tbsp tamari
- 2 tbsp light tahini

- 360ml (12fl oz/ 1½ cups) water
- 2 tbsp olive oil

Serves 4–6

Soak the goji berries in water for 30–60 minutes, then drain. Add the goji berries, kimchee, tamari and tahini to a high-speed blender and cover with 180ml (6fl oz/¾ cup) of water. Blend until smooth. Add the rest of the water and the olive oil and blend again.

WILD WISDOM

Depending on the variety of kimchee you use as a base, feel free to add additional spices, herbs (such as coriander) or medicinal mushroom extracts (such as reishi). Enjoy the soup cold, at room temperature, or with some warm 60–70°C/140–158°F water added.

PEAR AND CASHEW SOUP

When it comes to raw soups, comfort factor and a gourmet flavour are not always easy to attain. Mainly because raw ingredients are so 'alive' that they chemically interact with each other, creating unexpected flavour profiles that can sometimes be a bit off track. With that in mind, however, we made this recipe to deliver every time. It is one of our all-time favourite raw soups. It is easy-going, bursting with summery and autumnal flavours and is deliciously satisfying.

- 500ml (18fl oz/generous 2 cups) warm water
- juice of 1 lemon
- 1 fennel bulb, peeled and chopped
- 2 pears, peeled and chopped
- ¼ cauliflower, chopped
- 100g (3½oz/⅔ cup) soaked cashews
- 4 naturally cured pitted green olives
- 30g (1¼oz) Irish moss purée (optional)
- 5 spring onions (white ends only), or 1–2 small shallots
- 1 tbsp white miso
- 1–2 tbsp white/light wildcrafted honey or other liquid sweetener of your choice
- ½ tsp ground black pepper
- sea salt to taste
- 2 tbsp olive oil
- cordyceps (optional)
- lion's mane (optional)

TO SERVE
- fennel pollen (optional)
- finely chopped fennel or dill fronds (optional)
- fresh truffle (optional)
- drizzle of olive or truffle oil

● Serves 4–6

In a high-speed blender, blend the measured warm water and lemon juice, then add all the ingredients apart from the olive oil, cordyceps and lion's mane. Blend on high for 1–2 minutes until smooth. Strain through a chinois or muslin if your blender doesn't blend finely enough.

When smooth, add the olive oil and mix in the cordyceps and lion's mane, if using.

Serve with fennel pollen, fennel or dill fronds, fresh truffle if in season, and a drizzle of olive or truffle oil.

NO-BONE BROTH
(WILD SEAWEED BROTH)

There is a reason why most us crave some kind of salty, warm broth when we feel unwell – be it bone broth, chicken broth or miso soup. That is because of our craving for good-quality salt water to maintain a delicate balance of sodium and potassium in our bodies that brings about an immediate sense of wellness and recovery.

We created this recipe as a plant-based response to the bone broth trend. A combination of nutrient-rich seaweeds and olives together with a simple yet fragrant spice mix creates a rich broth that is deeply nourishing for all times of the year.

- 2 tbsp coconut oil
- 2 small shallots, finely chopped
- 2 cloves of garlic, finely chopped
- 1.25cm (½ inch) piece of chilli, finely chopped
- 1.25cm (½-inch) piece of fresh root ginger, finely chopped
- 1.25cm (½-inch) piece of fresh turmeric, finely chopped
- 1 strand of thyme, finely chopped
- 5–6 sage leaves, finely chopped
- 3–4 mint leaves, finely chopped
- pinch of salt
- 1 leek, finely chopped
- 1 carrot, finely chopped
- 8–10 naturally cured black olives, pitted and finely chopped
- 2–3 sticks of celery, finely chopped
- 60g (2oz) shiitake mushrooms, finely chopped (optional)
- 4 tbsp tamari
- 50g (1¾oz) dry sea spaghetti
- 40g (1½oz) dry wakame seaweed (or another seaweed)
- 2 litres (3½ pints/8 cups) filtered water
- 1–2 tbsp lime juice
- 2 tbsp unpasteurised miso

Preheat a heavy-bottomed saucepan and melt the coconut oil in it. Once hot, add the shallots, garlic, chilli, ginger, turmeric and fresh herbs. Sauté for a few minutes on a low heat. Then add the salt, leek, carrot, olives, celery and shiitake mushrooms, if using. Add the tamari and seaweeds. Stir well.

CONTINUED OVERLEAF

NO-BONE BROTH
(WILD SEAWEED BROTH) CONTINUED

TO SERVE
- lime
- fresh coriander
- chopped chilli
- pine nuts

● Serves 4–6

Add the measured water and heat until simmering. Simmer gently for a couple of hours, adding more water if necessary, then turn the heat off. Mix in the lime juice and miso and serve in bowls at around 60–80°C/140–176°F with a quarter of lime, coriander, chilli and pine nuts.

To make a thicker broth, take out some of the seaweed, place in a high-speed blender with enough broth liquid to cover the seaweed and blend until you get a smooth purée. Pour the purée back into the rest of the stock and stir to mix and thicken.

If you prefer to make a big batch of broth to use later or freeze, allow the broth to reduce to a concentrate over a very low heat. Then place all the contents in a blender and blend well until you get a thick cream. Upon defrosting use as a soup stock or enjoy as a broth by adding warm water, extra vegetables or herbs.

WILD WISDOM

The main talking point of bone broth is collagen – the beautifying type of protein that is used as a connective and supportive tissue throughout the body. Contrary to common belief, collagen is not actually directly absorbable by the body from consuming bone broth but is produced by the body from a selection of amino acids and vitamin C – all readily present in seaweed and leading-edge sources of plant protein.

IRISH MOSS AND TOMATO CEVICHE

This ceviche is our wild take on a Peruvian dish which traditionally features meat or fish. Ceviche lends itself wonderfully to plant-based cuisine. The key to the ceviche is the 'leche de tigre' marinade, which is rich in lime juice and spices. The natural acidity of the marinade helps break down or 'chemically cook' the raw ingredients, making them easier to digest, and also creates a spectrum of deep, delicious, refreshingly zingy flavours in the process. Serve with fresh blue corn tacos, raw crackers, freshly baked bread or just as it is.

- 10g (¼oz) Irish moss
- 30g (1¼oz) shiitake mushrooms
- 120ml (4fl oz/½ cup) tamari
- 300g (10½oz) tomatoes, chopped
- 25g (1oz) red onion, chopped
- 1 tbsp chopped coriander, plus extra to garnish
- 50g (1¾oz) tenderstem broccoli, thinly sliced
- 50g (1¾oz) red pepper, diced
- 1 tsp diced green chilli
- 2 tbsp lime juice
- 2 tbsp olive oil
- ½ tsp smoked paprika
- 300ml (10fl oz/1¼ cups) tomato juice
- 2 tsp salt
- 1 tsp ground black pepper

Serves 4–6

Soak the Irish moss in water overnight, then drain just before serving.

Thinly slice the shiitake mushrooms and marinate them in the tamari for 2 hours, then drain, reserving the tamari.

In a large non-metallic bowl, mix together the tomato, onion, coriander, broccoli, red pepper and green chilli. Mix in the lime juice, olive oil, smoked paprika, tomato juice and 2 tbsp of the reserved tamari sauce. Add salt and black pepper to taste. Mix well for 1–2 minutes then cover the bowl and leave in the fridge to marinate for 2 hours.

After 2 hours, remove from the fridge and leave at room temperature for 10 minutes. To serve, divide between bowls and sprinkle with Irish moss strands and chopped coriander.

CALIFORNIAN SUSHI ROLLS

Everybody loves sushi rolls. It seems to be a cornerstone of our modern interconnected lifestyle: the architecture of sushi is so adaptive to switching ingredients, local and dietary preferences, and lends itself to continuous improvisation. These sushi rolls are elegant, light and – once you get the hang of it – super creative and easy to prepare. Make as a snack for your lunch box or as a finger food option for a bigger gathering.

- 200g (7oz) oyster mushrooms, shredded
- 1 tbsp chopped coriander
- 2 spring onions, chopped
- juice of ½ lime
- ½ tbsp maple syrup
- 1 tbsp sesame oil
- ½ tbsp tamari, plus extra to serve
- 200g (7oz) cauliflower, cut into chunks
- 4 nori sheets
- 8 tsp Wasabi Aioli, plus extra to serve (see page 176)
- 1 avocado, thinly sliced
- ½ long cucumber, cut into thin strips
- 4 tbsp kimchee (see page 124)

Serves 2–4

Place the oyster mushrooms, coriander, spring onion, lime juice, maple syrup, sesame oil and tamari in a bowl and toss to mix well. Place the mushroom mixture on a dehydrator sheet and dehydrate at 42–45°C/107–113°F for 30 minutes. Turn the dehydrator sheet so that the back is now at the front and dehydrate for another 30 minutes or until the mushrooms are slightly tender and 'sticky'.

CONTINUED OVERLEAF

CALIFORNIAN SUSHI ROLLS CONTINUED

Blend the cauliflower in a food processor until a 'rice-like' consistency. Avoid over-blending so it doesn't get too creamy or powdery.

Place a nori sheet on a bamboo mat and spread on 2 tsp of Wasabi Aioli, making a horizontal line and leaving 2cm (¾ inch) from the closest edge. Add 2 tbsp of cauliflower rice on top of the Wasabi Aioli line. Put 4 slices of avocado, 4 cucumber strips, 1 tbsp of kimchee and 1 tbsp of marinated, slightly caramelised oyster mushrooms on top. Roll up the filled nori sheet firmly, pushing the bamboo mat back every time you roll to make a tight roll. When there's only around 2cm (¾ inch) left, spread a little water on the end edge to make it stick to the roll and seal. Repeat with the other 3 nori sheets and fillings.

Cut each roll into 6 pieces and serve with tamari sauce and extra Wasabi Aioli.

SUMMER GODDESS BOWL

Quality seasonal ingredients and good combinations are always a winner when it comes to everyday food. The Summer Goddess bowl was a simple idea of showcasing our favourite seasonal ingredients all in one bowl, but turned into one of our bestselling dishes of the summer.

CUCUMBER AND PEPPER SALAD

– 200g (7oz) red pepper, diced
– 200g (7oz) cucumber, diced
– 3 diced gherkins
– ⅓ red onion, diced
– 1 tsp salt
– 1 tsp lemon juice
– 2 tbsp chopped dill

MARINATED TOMATOES

– 350g (10½oz) diced heritage tomatoes
– 1 tsp salt
– ⅓ tsp ground black pepper
– 1 tbsp chopped garlic leaf or 1 small clove of garlic, diced
– 1 tbsp diced shallots

PEA MASH

– 250g (9oz) frozen or fresh peas
– ½ tsp salt
– pinch of ground black pepper
– 3 tbsp olive oil
– 15 mint leaves

COCONUT AND PINE NUT CHEESE SAUCE

– 70g (2½oz/½ cup) pine nuts
– 120ml (4fl oz/½ cup) coconut water
– 40g (1½oz/½ cup) nutritional yeast
– pinch of salt
– ½ tsp turmeric powder

CAULI 'N' CHEESE

– 100g (3½oz/1 cup) cauliflower florets
– 2 tbsp Coconut and Pine Nut Cheese Sauce (see left)

TO ASSEMBLE, PER PORTION

– 1 tsp sunflower oil
– 50g (1¾oz/½ cup) mixed sprouts
– pinch of salt
– ½ avocado, sliced
– 1 tsp chopped chives
– a small handful of fresh pea-shoots or other baby greens

CONTINUED OVERLEAF

SUMMER GODDESS BOWL CONTINUED

● **Serves 2–4**

First make the Coconut and Pine Nut Cheese Sauce by blending all the sauce ingredients together in a high-speed blender until smooth.

Mix all the Cucumber and Pepper Salad ingredients in a bowl and set aside. Mix all the Marinated Tomatoes ingredients in a bowl and set aside.

To make the Pea Mash, defrost the peas first if using frozen peas. Blanch the peas in boiling water for 40 seconds then rinse under cold water. Place in a food processor and pulse with the rest of the Pea Mash ingredients.

Break the cauliflower florets into small 2.5–4cm (1–1½ inch) pieces and blanch in boiling water for 1 minute, then rinse under cold water. In a bowl mix the cauliflower with 2 tbsp of the Coconut and Pine Nut Cheese Sauce.

In a frying pan, heat the sunflower oil, add the sprouts and salt and toss to heat through.

To serve, place a portion of the Cauli Cheese, warm sprouts, Cucumber and Pepper Salad, Marinated Tomatoes and Pea Mash in a bowl and top with the sliced avocado. Sprinkle chopped chives on top of the cauliflower, add some fresh pea-shoots or other leaves, and serve.

STUFFED FIGS WRAPPED IN COCONUT BACON

When figs are in season (from July until about September), we seek them out, buy a big box of juicy, soft, ripe and jammy ones and devour them in one sitting.

- 120g (4oz) mixed baby
  leaf salad
- 2 tbsp Mustard Dressing
  (see page 144)
- 6–8 large, ripe figs
- 4 tbsp naturally cured pitted
  olives, such as kalamata
- sprinkle of fresh peas

COCONUT BACON
- 200g (7oz/2½ cups) young
  coconut meat
- 3 tbsp BBQ Sauce
  (see page 176)

CREAM CHEESE
- 100g (3½oz/⅓ cup)
  coconut cream
- ½ tsp turmeric powder
- 1 probiotic capsule
- 100ml (3½fl oz/scant ½ cup)
  tinned coconut milk
- 1 tsp salt
- 1 tbsp nutritional yeast
- juice of ½ lime

Serves 2

To make the Coconut Bacon, start by slicing the coconut meat into thin sheets. Mix the coconut sheets with the BBQ Sauce and let it marinate for 3–4 hours. Place on a dehydrator sheet and dehydrate at 45°C/113°F for 1½ hours. Flip the sheets around and dehydrate for another 1½ hours until the coconut bacon is semi-dry, yet not crunchy.

To make the Cream Cheese, place the coconut cream sachet or jar in hot water and leave to melt for around 15 minutes. Add all the ingredients to a high-speed blender and blend until smooth. Transfer to a piping bag and keep in the freezer.

To assemble the dish, put the salad leaves in a mixing bowl and add the Mustard Dressing. Mix thoroughly and place in the middle of the plate. Make a cross cut in the top of the figs and fill them with the Cream Cheese. Wrap with Coconut Bacon and place on top of the salad. To decorate, add the olives and whole peas.

SEARED POLENTA WITH TOMATOES AND ASPARAGUS

This dish has become an iconic special at the Wild Food Café and our team meals. Put together by our head chef, Thet, it celebrates seasonality, rich tomato-y flavours, and the irresistible golden crispiness of polenta, yet it is totally unpretentious and provides plenty of comfort. It hits all the right notes ... and for that reason, we are sharing it with you.

- 800ml (28fl oz/3⅓ cups) water
- pinch of salt
- 200g (7oz) polenta
- 15g (½oz/3 tbsp) nutritional yeast
- 6–12 asparagus spears

- 1 tbsp sunflower oil
- microgreens or chopped coriander, to garnish

SAUTEÉD TOMATOES
- 2 tbsp sunflower oil
- 1 tbsp shallots, chopped

- 1 tsp garlic, chopped
- 150g (5½oz) cherry tomatoes, halved
- 3 tbsp water
- pinch of salt and pepper
- 5g (⅛oz) samphire
- 1 tsp parsley, chopped

● Serves 2–4

It is best to prepare the polenta the day before. To make the polenta, bring the measured water and salt to a boil in a saucepan. When the water is boiling, slowly add the polenta, constantly stirring with a wooden spoon. Cook on a medium heat for 5–8 minutes, stirring, until you see it start to thicken. Mix in the nutritional yeast, stir, and remove from the heat. Grease a rectangular 25–27cm tray and evenly pour the polenta into the tray. Let it sit in the fridge for 6 hours until firm.

To make the Sautéed Tomatoes, heat the sunflower oil in a frying pan and cook the shallots and garlic until translucent. Add the cherry tomatoes to the frying pan, then add the measured water and salt and pepper and cook for around 1 minute. Add the samphire and parsley, toss, and remove from the heat.

Blanch the asparagus in boiling water for 30 seconds, then
drain. Cut the polenta into squares. Heat the sunflower oil in a
frying pan and add the polenta. Cook for 1½ minutes on each
side until it becomes golden and crispy on the outside.

Place the sautéed tomatoes in the middle of the plate, then
add the asparagus and place the polenta on top. Add a garnish
of microgreens or fresh coriander to finish.

KING OYSTER SCALLOPS

For lovers of mushrooms and all things umami, this dish is an absolute superstar. Sometimes we marinate the oyster mushrooms in advance (as per the recipe), prepare the sauces to go with it, and take it with us to the wild to finish it off on the open fire. It really is the best way to enjoy this dish.

- 120ml (4fl oz/½ cup) tamari
- 1 tsp rosemary, chopped
- ½ tsp ground black pepper
- 120ml (4fl oz/½ cup) olive oil

- 1 tsp salt
- 2 cloves of garlic, chopped
- 1 tbsp wakame seaweed

- 600g (1lb 5oz) king oyster mushrooms
- 1 tbsp sunflower oil

TO SERVE
- 1 nori sheet
- 2 tbsp Garlic Mayonnaise (see page 181)
- 2 tbsp Tomato Salsa (see page 182)
- 8 leaves of sea purslane (optional)

● Serves 2–4

Combine all the ingredients apart from the mushrooms and sunflower oil in a medium-sized bowl.

Chop the oyster mushrooms into thick 2.5cm (1-inch) slices and toss in the sauce. Let them marinate for 30 minutes.

Heat the sunflower oil in a non-stick frying pan over a medium heat and cook the mushrooms for 90 seconds on each side. Toast the nori sheet over a gas hob flame or in a dry frying pan being careful not to burn it.

To serve, place dollops of Garlic Mayonnaise on the plate and place the mushrooms on top. Spoon Tomato Salsa on top. Break and crumble the nori sheet and add it along with the sea purslane, if using, on top of the mushrooms.

CALL OF THE WILD

Nettle is one of the most prolific wild medicinal and culinary greens in the Northern Hemisphere. You can find pristine patches of nettle popping up pretty much in every garden, park or forest. Alternatively, farmers' markets and some health food shops stock wild nettle throughout the spring and summer.

- 380g (13oz/2 cups) quinoa
- 960ml (32fl oz/4 cups) boiling water
- 2 tbsp coriander seeds
- 2 tbsp fennel seeds
- 2 tbsp white sesame seeds
- pinch of salt
- 1 nori sheet
- 8–10 asparagus spears
- 2 tbsp sunflower oil
- 10g (¼oz/1½ cups) nettle leaves
- ½ tsp ground black pepper
- 2 tbsp Coconut and Pine Nut Cheese Sauce (see page 81)
- Small handful of wild wood sorrel or sorrel, to garnish

Serves 2

Boil the quinoa and measured water in a medium-sized saucepan over a high heat for 15 minutes. Drain and rinse under cold water. Let the quinoa sit for 5 minutes and then toss it to make sure it is not wet at all.

In a frying pan, toast the coriander and fennel seeds over a medium heat for 40–50 seconds until the spices become fragrant. Transfer them to a bowl then toast the sesame seeds for 40–50 seconds. Put all the seeds together in a spice grinder with a pinch of salt, and then grind them until you break the seeds (not too fine, nor too coarse). Transfer to a separate bowl.

Cut the nori sheet into small pieces and add to the bowl with the spice mix.

Blanch the asparagus in salted boiling water for 40–50 seconds, rinse under cold water and set aside.

In a heavy-bottomed skillet, heat the sunflower oil over a medium heat. Add the quinoa and nettles and cook until the nettle is wilted, about 1–3 minutes.

Once ready, place the quinoa and nettle mix in the middle of each plate, put 4–5 asparagus spears on top, then drizzle with the Coconut and Pine Nut Cheese Sauce. Sprinkle with the spice and nori mix, add a twist of freshly ground black pepper and garnish with some chopped sorrel or wild wood sorrel.

FLOW

WATER

ENVIRONMENT

Water is the spirit of the West, which can be called upon (by facing this direction) to be in touch with the flow of our feelings. To purify, cleanse and restore our natural innocence, vitality and youthfulness. Healing means to become whole, finding relief and letting go of the old. When we are 'in flow' we become the masters of our emotional – and correspondingly physical wellbeing.

This is the time of autumnal harvest, where the slowing of rapid growth allows us to grasp and attain what has become ripe, as old leaves are dropped. This element is moist in its essence and carries a sweet flavour spectrum. It is the afternoon transforming into the evening towards the sunset. In our bodies, water rules all the fluids, including the tears. Symbolically, it is represented by the black bear, plant and herbal medicines and dark-coloured (blue and black) crystals such as obsidian and onyx. It is associated with the cleansing and purifying aroma of sage smoke. It is the waning moon.

We know of our intrinsic responsibility to keep the waters pure and to take care of the springs, rivers, the lakes and oceans. More often than not it seems a daunting task that is way beyond our control. Although we can just as easily remember that the most immediate waters are inside us. Taking care of our internal waters, a whole 70–75 per cent of our beautiful bodies, opens infinite possibilities for our everyday thriving.

With that in mind, treat yourself well. Drink plenty of water. We recommend 3–4 litres a day, depending on your levels of activity, ideally drinking 750–1000ml before breakfast, and the same again halfway between breakfast and lunch, between lunch and dinner, and again between dinner and bedtime. Eat plenty of hydrating raw, fresh foods, think inspiring thoughts, carry good intentions, be kind and gentle to yourself and your loved ones and your internal waters will reflect that, creating a ripple effect in your immediate and extended environment.

RITUALS

HYDRATION MEDITATION

Every time you raise a glass of water to
your lips, make a micro meditation out of it.
Acknowledge that this water will eternally
and infinitely pass its way across the whole
Earth ecosystem, assuming different qualities
and identities. If you are feeling tired, invoke
vitality. Shake the bottle, spin the water or
glass in a vortex or stir it with a wooden spoon.
Feel the liveliness of its flow and then drink
that water. It will have an effect on your state.

If you are feeling lonely and disconnected,
remember and feel that that water is
connected to all the water in the world, and
therefore connects all of us. When we really
feel that connection and feel the water in our
mouths, we feel how easily and effortlessly
it melts, merges and transforms with us and
into us. When you are feeling that you are
lacking anything in your life, remember the
abundance of water. This planet is two-thirds
water; we are surrounded by an immeasurable
ocean. Feeling the magnitude of this, feeling
how water flows is the greatest teaching of
abundance.

Whichever water we are lucky enough to be
drinking and refreshing ourselves with, it is
only as amazing as we allow it to be through
the alchemy of appreciation. Our first priority
is to be thankful that we have this gift of
water every time we drink it, knowing that
some people may have had to walk many
miles for a single drop.

YOUTH ELIXIR

We all come from water, spending nine
months in the waters of the womb before
entering this world. In water we get back
to our primal natural state of youthfulness,
innocence and vitality. Water is naturally
rejuvenating, beautifying and regenerative: it
has a natural medicinal quality, as long as we
remember to be conscious of it.

Seas and oceans are natural mineral baths, so
whenever you have an opportunity, immerse
yourself in the healing waters of the ocean – it
is the best ritual bath you will ever have. Take
ritual baths and showers with an intention to
purify, cleanse and rejuvenate not just your
body, but your mind and emotions as well.
Add fresh flowers, natural scents and salts and
create an environment that is restorative to
you. Remind yourself of the reflective nature
of water and use it to consciously wash away
the burdens, stresses and pollution of everyday
life and to bring yourself back to your natural,
connected state of youthful thriving.

💧 Wild practice: wild bath infusion

Whenever you don't have ocean at your doorstep, create a mini ocean with a wild bath infusion at home.

- 50g dry seaweed of your choice, such as kelp or Irish moss
- 150g–1kg Dead Sea minerals or other natural sea salt
- 150g–1kg magnesium chloride flakes
- few drops of organic essential oil: choose from rosemary, geranium, rose, jasmine, lavender, chamomile, lemon, pine, frankincense, cypress, blue yarrow, fir, sandalwood, eucalyptus
- 25–50ml carrier oil: choose from rosehip, cacao, almond, coconut, sesame
- handful of fresh or dried flowers: chamomile, lavender, jasmine, rose, cornflower, hibiscus, magnolia, marigold
- crystals of your choice (make sure the crystals are not water-soluble), such as quartz family, amethysts, carnelian or a selection of simple beach pebbles.

Start by blending the seaweed with double the amount of water to make a smooth purée. Add more water if necessary for blending. Once smooth, creamy and runny enough, pour the seaweed mix into the running bath. Add the dead sea minerals and magnesium flakes (the quantity you add will determine how strong and medicinal you want your bath to be, so experiment with a quantity that works for you).

Mix a selection of organic essential oils into the carrier oil, then pour into the bath together with the dried or fresh flowers just before getting in. Place crystals inside the bath or hold them in your hands. Use a smoke of sage, palo santo or juniper to smudge yourself of all static and negativity accumulated during the day and light a candle to create a ritual environment where all the elements are present. Immerse yourself in the bath for 20–30 minutes in deep peace and enjoy the wild glow afterwards.

CONNECT TO WILD WATER

Springs within our ecosystem are the source of life as the fresh purified and matured water from deep in Mother Earth's belly overflows with ripeness at these particular points on Earth. To connect more with nature, it is an awesome practice to start visiting wild springs or other natural water sources from time to time. It is like a mini pilgrimage to wild paradise and can be especially beneficial when you are feeling stuck in any emotional states, or have 'hit the wall'. Inevitably, you will feel renewed, regenerated and at peace after visiting a spring. Appreciate and beautify the place upon arrival, picking up any litter, meditating there, singing a song, spending a few minutes in contemplation, washing your face and/or body or building a mini altar of rocks, leaves, flowers and shells.

Water is closely ruled by the moon, which happens to affect our bodies too. Start noticing when the full and new moon come, journal and write down your state and events during those days. The moon is known for its cyclical effect on every creature's behaviour on Earth, as well as the Earth's tides. It serves us greatly to pay attention to the moon's waxing and waning and its ever-changing effect on us and all of life.

HO' OPONOPONO

Our emotional wellbeing or 'flow' is closely
linked to our ability to forgive and let go.
Try the powerful Hawaiian practice of
Ho'oponopono, which roughly translates as
to put right, correct or rectify. It allows our
emotions to flow and be like water, which
is at the core of our emotional, mental and
physical health. It is a remarkably simple
and powerful tool for realising radical
responsibility for all aspects of our life
experience. Ho'oponopono was made famous
through the work of Dr Hew Len of Hawaii,
where he used it to heal a whole ward of
'violent and criminally insane' patients.
The process involves simply repeating the
phrase 'I am sorry, please forgive me, I love
you, thank you' to ourselves and to others
with an intention to restore and resettle our
perception of ourselves and our world
into what feels right.

The forgiveness practice always starts with
ourselves first, as forgiveness can only radiate
from inside out. When we can forgive
ourselves for thinking and judging that
we are wrong in the first place, we can be
at peace with the fact that each of us is
simply doing our best.

EDIBLES

Reconnect to the element of water and the season of autumn by making your own food medicines: your personalised provisions for winter: from fermented goods, other pantry preparations, or the great medicine of sweetness in a form of mouth-watering desserts. Not by chance, both fermented foods and desserts are considered as the most soul-infused foods.

Sweet desserts and fermented provisions are perfectly condusive to being combined with more medicinal foods and flavours. After all, in nature every wild fruit's sweetness of flesh is complemented with hints of sourness and bitterness in their leaves, pith, rind, skin and seeds. Sweetness is known to be a perfect medicine carrier, opening the cells of our bodies for the medicine to be absorbed and delivered. Experiment by adding wild foods, bitter foods, sour foods and herbs (especially spices) to your sweet desserts to bring out more medicinal qualities; try infusing them with reishi, baobab, rosehip, nettle, maca, goji berries, seaweeds, medicinal mushroom extracts, spirulina or juniper berries. This will bring satiation, medicinal functionality and a spectrum of unique flavours to the forefront of your kitchen alchemy. Desserts made in this way not only give us the bliss of sweetness, but they do so in such a way that is not corrupted by the guilt of refined sugars, and their accompanying numbing energy crash.

When it comes to food in general, in autumn and winter, we love comforting soups, stews, warming lattes, some pseudo-grains (such as quinoa, amaranth and wild rice), an abundance of squashes, fermented foods and salads with some cooked components and root vegetables in play.

RAW CHOCOLATE TART

This iconic recipe is one of only a few that has been on our menu at the Wild Food Café from day one. It remains on the menu by popular demand and we can't imagine it any other way. It no longer belongs to us ... it belongs to everyone who has ever tasted it, enjoyed it or shared it with their friends. It is the raw chocolate tart of the wild extended family. Nut-free too!

TART BASE
- 85g (3oz/½ cup) chopped dates
- 40g (1½oz/½ cup) coconut flakes
- 1 tbsp coconut oil, melted
- 30g (1¼oz/¼ cup) cacao powder
- ½ tbsp maple syrup
- ½ tbsp vanilla extract

TART FILLING
- 2 avocados
- 2 tbsp mesquite powder
- 125g (4oz/1 cup) coconut sugar
- 120g (4oz/1 cup) cacao powder
- 100g (3½oz/½ cup) coconut oil
- 200ml (7fl oz/generous ¾ cup) coconut milk
- 60ml (2fl oz/¼ cup) maple syrup
- ½ tbsp vanilla extract
- pinch of salt

● **Serves 2–4**

Place all the base ingredients in a food processor and blend until you get a crumbly, sticky texture. Press the dough down into a 21cm (8-inch) cake tin, making sure it is as even as possible. Chill in the fridge for 15 minutes while you prepare the filling.

Blend all the filling ingredients in a food processor or high-speed blender until smooth, then transfer to the cake tin and smooth over the base. Allow to set in the fridge for 6 hours before serving. To serve, dust with some cacao powder or use Chocolate Sauce (see page 28), fresh edible flowers and berries.

WILD DOUGHNUTS

This recipe won over our hearts. Instantly. It is super decadent (especially when coated in raw chocolate) and with a variety of toppings will make any table look absolutely gorgeous.

- 2 apples
- 2 tbsp agave or maple syrup
- 120ml (4fl oz/½ cup) almond milk
- 1 tbsp apple cider vinegar
- 185g (6½oz/1½ cups) coconut sugar
- 80ml (3fl oz/⅓ cup) melted coconut oil
- 25g (1oz/¼ cup) gram flour

- 190g (6¾oz/1¾ cups) gluten-free flour
- 1½ tsp baking powder
- ½ tsp bicarbonate of soda
- 1 tsp vanilla essence
- 1 tsp ground cinnamon
- pinch of salt

TOPPING
- Raw Chocolate (see page 108)
- Coconut Cream
- Granola Clusters (see page 55)
- fresh berries
- flower petals
- flaked hazelnuts and pistachio nuts
- finely chopped coconut flakes

● **Serves 2–4**

Preheat the oven to 170°C/325°F/Gas Mark 3.

Blend the apples and agave or maple syrup in a high-speed blender to make a smooth apple sauce.

Mix all the other doughnut ingredients with the apple sauce and fill the holes of a doughnut silicone mould until they are about three-quarters full. Set aside for 30 minutes so that the dough rises, then bake in the preheated oven for 25 minutes.

Remove from the oven and allow to cool on a baking rack. Once cool, dip in melted Raw Chocolate, decorate with Coconut Cream and toppings of your choice and place on a baking rack to set.

PISTACHIO LOLLY

The prerequisite of any phenomenal dessert is that it is delicious and irresistibly beautiful. The vibration of beauty on a plate will nourish you and your loved ones on many levels and will be a definite hit with children.

- 65g (2oz/⅓ cup) coconut oil
- 40g (1½oz/⅓ cup) soaked cashew nuts, drained
- 65ml (2½fl oz/¼ cup) agave syrup
- 120ml (4fl oz/½ cup) coconut milk (from a carton, not tinned)
- 2 tsp vanilla extract

- pinch of salt
- 125ml (4fl oz/½ cup) tinned coconut milk
- 110g (3¾oz/¾ cup) skinless pistachios
- 1 tbsp lemon juice
- 1 tsp sunflower lecithin
- 15g (½oz/½ cup) baby spinach

TO COAT
- 120g (4oz/½ cup) cacao butter
- 25ml (1fl oz/5 tsp) agave syrup
- ¼ tsp sunflower lecithin
- 40g (1½oz/¼ cup) chopped pistachios

Makes 12–14 lollies

Blend all the lolly ingredients apart from the baby spinach in a high-speed blender until smooth. Let it sit for 10 minutes until the jug is not warm anymore, then add the spinach and blend again – try not to over-blend. Pour the liquid into silicone lolly moulds so they are half filled and put a wooden ice-cream stick in each. Place in the freezer for 20 minutes, then fill each lolly mould up to the top and place in the freezer for 4 hours until firm.

Chop the cacao butter and place in a stainless-steel bowl with the agave and sunflower lecithin. Place the bowl over a saucepan of simmering water and stir until fully melted.

Take the lollies out of the moulds and dip them in the melted cacao butter. Remove, wait 5 seconds and dip them again. As soon as you take them out the second time, sprinkle a teaspoon of chopped pistachios on top. Freeze prior to serving. Serve with fresh berries and some raw granola clusters or just as it is.

WATERMELON AND STRAWBERRY ICE CREAM

An easy-to-make but totally lush and unforgettable ice cream you can enjoy at home. Perfect for the first warm and sunny days of summer.

- 100g (3½oz) creamed coconut
- 50g (1¾oz/¼ cup) extra virgin coconut oil, melted
- 60g (2oz/½ cup) coconut sugar
- 150g (5½oz) frozen young coconut flesh
- 10g (¼oz) strawberry powder or freeze- dried strawberries
- 200g (7oz) frozen strawberries
- ½ tsp vanilla extract or fresh vanilla seeds
- 80g (2¾oz) frozen watermelon

Serves 2–4

In a high-speed blender, blend the creamed coconut, coconut oil and coconut sugar until you get a smooth, creamy mix. Add the frozen coconut flesh and blend while mixing the ingredients vigorously with a tamper or push stick. Make sure not to over-blend and keep the frozen coconut as cold as possible, especially if you are intending to serve the ice cream right away.

Add the strawberry powder and frozen strawberries and blend again using the push stick until all the ingredients are mixed in. Finally, add the vanilla extract and frozen watermelon and blend again for a few moments.

We recommend preparing the ice cream in advance, freezing it for a few hours and sticking it in a food processor or blender for a few moments before serving to achieve a fluffy, creamy texture.

SWEET AVOCADO EGGS

Joel: 'When avocado and cacao are present you know things are going well. Both are aphrodisiac medicinal foods with luxurious qualities, so it almost doesn't matter which way you choose to combine them, or whether you choose a sweet or savoury direction, the results are always lush and delicious. In this recipe the relationship of avocado and cacao is as deconstructed as it gets. For me it was a way to recreate a memory of a Feast ice cream with crunchy chocolate on the outside, soft filling inside and more chocolate in the middle.'

– 2–3 large or 4–5 small avocados

RAW CHOCOLATE
– 100g (3½oz/1 cup) grated raw cacao liquor/paste
– 55g (1¾oz/¼ cup) grated cacao butter

– 40g (1½oz/⅓ cup) coconut palm sugar
– pinch of salt
– 1 tbsp of your favourite wild superfood or tonic herb extract (optional)

FILLING
– 65g (2¼oz/¼ cup) soaked dried mango
– 2 tbsp melted creamed coconut
– 3 tbsp coconut sugar
– 3g (⅛oz) ground ginger

Makes 6–10 portions

First, place the unpeeled avocados in the fridge. It will be easier to pour chocolate on them if they are cold.

To make the Raw Chocolate, melt the raw cacao liquor and cacao butter using a double-boiler or bain-marie. Stir in the coconut palm sugar, salt and your favourite wild superfood or tonic herb, if using.

To make the filling, put the soaked mango with a little bit of the mango soaking water, melted creamed coconut, coconut sugar and ginger into a high-speed blender. Blend until you get a smooth cream, using a tamper or push stick if necessary.

Take the avocados out of the fridge, peel them whole and carefully cut each avocado in half. Take the pits out, stuff the holes with the mango filling and place them flat side down on a ceramic or wooden board or plate.

Pour the Raw Chocolate onto the avocado halves, decorate with your choice of ingredients (rose petals, flaked almonds, coconut chips) and place in the fridge to set. Once set, you can pour a second layer of raw chocolate on top to get a thicker chocolate layer if you wish.

BLACKBERRY CHEESECAKE

The inspiration behind this decadent raw cheesecake is a humble wild blackberry. With wild blackberries so abundantly available in England and most of the Northern Hemisphere in autumn, when most other fruits are already out of season, we had to create a dessert to do it justice. This cheesecake definitely delivers with a captivating colour and creamy decadence. Thank you blackberries and all things wild!

BASE
- 110g (3¾oz/1½ cups) coconut flakes
- 40g (1½oz/¼ cup) buckwheat
- 70g (2½oz/½ cup) sunflower seeds
- 75g (2¾oz/½ cup) pumpkin seeds
- 120ml (4fl oz/½ cup) maple syrup
- 2 tbsp maca
- 220g (8oz/2 cups) broken pecans
- ¼ tsp vanilla paste

FILLING
- 5g (⅛oz) Irish moss
- 135ml (4½fl oz/generous ½ cup) maple syrup
- 80ml (3fl oz/⅓ cup) lemon juice
- 160g (5¾oz/¾ cup) soaked cashews, drained
- ⅛ tsp salt
- ⅛ tsp vanilla paste
- 65g (2¼oz/⅓ cup) coconut oil
- 165g (6oz/generous 1 cup) blackberries

TO DECORATE
- crumbled pecans
- raspberries
- blackberries
- microgreens, such as lemon verbena or mint
- edible flowers

● **Makes 11 small or 1 large cheesecake**

To make the base, blend all the ingredients together in a food processor until fine. Grease 11 small cake rings or a 21cm (8-inch) cake ring with coconut oil. Line a tray with baking paper and place the cake ring(s) on top.

Fill each ring with 2 tbsp of the base mixture (or fill the large cake tin with all the mix) and press it down. Let it sit in the fridge for 10 minutes while you make the filling.

To make the filling, start by blending the Irish moss, maple syrup and lemon juice in a high-speed blender until it reaches a custard-like consistency – make sure the texture is not grainy. Add the cashews, salt and vanilla and blend until smooth. Add the coconut oil and blackberries and blend again until smooth.

CONTINUED OVERLEAF

BLACKBERRY CHEESECAKE CONTINUED

Take the tray out of the fridge and fill the cake ring(s) to the top with the filling. Chill in the freezer for 2–3 hours.

Before serving, remove the cake ring(s) and let the cheesecake defrost for 20 minutes. To serve, decorate with crumbled pecans, fresh raspberries and blackberries, microgreens and/or edible flower petals.

WILD WISDOM

Irish moss — a wild seaweed — adds lightness, fluffiness, volume and an abundance of trace minerals to desserts. It is neutral in colour and flavour and therefore has myriad applications in raw dessert preparation.

MOSSY MATCHA CHEESECAKE

It is well known that a sweet flavour is used as a delivery vehicle for the medicinal (often bitter) components to reach our cells. Use the architecture of this cheesecake recipe to create a delicious medicinal dessert for you and your loved ones. Whenever we have an opportunity to make a green cake, we use it to add extra medicinal goodness to the recipe by adding green powders, herbs or other tonics.

BASE
- 175g (6¼oz/generous 1 cup) dates
- 140g (5oz/1 cup) almonds
- 75g (2¾oz/1 cup) coconut flakes
- 1 tbsp mesquite (optional)
- 1 tsp dried nettle root powder (optional)

FOR MEDICINAL FACTOR
(optional)
- 1 tsp he-shou-wu extract or any spice/tonic herb of your choice
- 1 tsp medicinal mushroom extracts
- 2 tbsp barley grass powder

FILLING
- 195g (7oz/1½ cups) soaked cashews
- 240ml (8fl oz/1 cup) coconut milk
- 240ml (8fl oz/1 cup) agave syrup
- juice of 1 lemon
- 175g (6¼oz/2 cups) coconut meat
- 1 tbsp vanilla extract
- 105g (3½oz/½ cup) coconut oil
- 1 tsp sunflower lecithin
- ⅛ tsp salt
- 2 tbsp matcha powder

TO DECORATE
- matcha powder
- microgreens such as lemon verbena or mint

● Makes 9 small or 1 large cheesecake

First soak the dates in warm water for 5 minutes, then drain. To make the base, blend all the base ingredients together in the food processor until fine. If adding the medicinal factor and using darker tonic herb powders such as he-shou-wu or medicinal mushroom extracts, mix them into the base so they do not affect the colour of the filling. (If using barley grass powder, add to the filling.)

CONTINUED OVERLEAF

MOSSY MATCHA CHEESECAKE
CONTINUED

Grease 9 small cake rings or a 21cm (8-inch) cake ring with coconut oil. Line a tray with baking paper and place the cake ring(s) on top.

Fill each small cake ring with 2 tbsp of the base mixture (or the large one with all the base mix) and press down. Let it sit in the fridge for 10 minutes while you make the filling.

To make the filling, blend all the filling ingredients apart from the matcha powder in a high-speed blender until smooth. Add the matcha powder and barley grass powder, if using, and give it a quick blend.

Take the tray out of the fridge and pour the filling into the cake ring(s). Chill in the freezer for 2–3 hours.

Before serving, remove the cake ring(s) and let the cheesecake defrost for 20 minutes. To decorate, dust with matcha powder and add microgreens such as lemon verbena or mint.

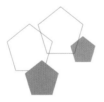

LEMON CHEESECAKE WITH SEA BUCKTHORN WHIRL

Sea buckthorn is one of the most prolific native superfoods and wild foods. It is packed with vitamin C and beneficial omega oils. Being super tangy, it works really well with all things zingy and lemony, perfectly complementing this classic lemon cheesecake.

BASE
- 175g (6¼oz/1 cup) dates
- 140g (5oz/1 cup) almonds
- 75g (2¾oz/1 cup) coconut flakes
- 1 tbsp mesquite

FILLING
- 40g (1½oz) Irish moss
- 360ml (12fl oz/1½ cups) agave syrup

- 1 tbsp lemon zest
- 360ml (12fl oz/1½ cups) lemon juice
- 120g (4oz/1½ cups) fresh coconut meat
- 260g (9¼oz/2 cups) soaked cashews, drained
- 1 tsp vanilla paste
- pinch of salt
- 315g (11oz/1½ cups) coconut oil

SEA BUCKTHORN SAUCE
- 125g (4oz/½ cup) goji berries
- 240ml (8fl oz/1 cup) sea buckthorn juice
- 480ml (16fl oz/2 cups) apple juice
- 240ml (8fl oz/1 cup) agave syrup

TO DECORATE
- edible flower petals

● **Makes 12 small or 1 large cheesecake**

Soak the Irish moss in water overnight, then drain.

Soak the dates in warm water for 5 minutes, then drain. To make the base, blend all the base ingredients together in a food processor until fine.

Grease 12 small or a 21cm (8-inch) cake tin with coconut oil. Line a tray with baking paper and place the cake ring(s) on top. Press the crust into the tin(s) making a small lip up the side. Let it sit in the fridge for 10 minutes while you make the filling.

CONTINUED OVERLEAF

LEMON CHEESECAKE WITH SEA BUCKTHORN WHIRL CONTINUED

To make the filling, blend the Irish moss, agave, lemon zest and lemon juice in a high-speed blender until it reaches a custard-like consistency – make sure the texture is not grainy. Add the coconut meat and blend until smooth. Add the cashews, vanilla and salt and blend until smooth. Add the coconut oil and give it a final blend. Pour the mixture into the cake tin(s).

Make the Sea Buckthorn Sauce. Soak the goji berries for 10 minutes in warm water, then drain. Blend all the sauce ingredients in a high-speed blender until the goji berries are well processed and the texture is smooth.

Drizzle 4 tbsp of the Sea Buckthorn Sauce on top of the cake, creating your own pattern. Let the cheesecake chill in the freezer for 2 hours.

Before serving, remove the cake tin(s) and let it defrost for 20 minutes. Decorate with edible flowers if you wish.

WILD WISDOM

Mesquite powder, or white carob, adds a wonderful biscuit-like flavour to raw desserts. If you don't have mesquite powder handy, you can omit it altogether; or replace with lucuma powder for an additional layer of mildly sweet creaminess; baobab powder for a tangy lemony edge; or brown carob powder for a dark base and a mild caramel flavour.

UPSIDE-DOWN CHESTNUT AND PINE NUT PIE

This upside-down pie appeared on our winter menu one year and remained forever imprinted in our hearts. The combination of caramelised raisins, chestnuts and pine nuts is absolutely heavenly.

TOPPING
- 200g (7oz) boiled chestnuts, roughly chopped
- 30g (1¼oz/¼ cup) pine nuts
- 30g (1¼oz) soaked raisins, drained

CARAMEL
- 100g (3½oz) boiled chestnuts, roughly chopped
- 80g (2¾oz/⅔ cup) coconut sugar
- 30g (1¼oz/¼ cup) pine nuts
- 2 tbsp coconut oil
- 4 tbsp water

WET INGREDIENTS FOR THE PIE
- 280ml (9½fl oz/scant 1¼ cups) almond milk
- 240ml (8fl oz/1 cup) maple syrup
- 110g (3¾oz/½ cup) coconut sugar
- 100ml (3½fl oz/scant ½ cup) olive oil
- 1 stalk of rosemary, leaves only
- 1½ tbsp apple cider vinegar
- zest of 2 oranges
- ½ tsp salt

DRY INGREDIENTS FOR THE PIE
- 230g (8oz/2 cups) gluten-free flour
- 40g (1½oz/⅓ cup) chestnut flour
- 30g (1¼oz/¼ cup) almond flour
- 100g (3½oz) boiled chestnuts
- 30g (1¼oz/scant ¼ cup) raisins
- 30g (1¼oz/¼ cup) pine nuts
- 2 tsp baking powder

TO DECORATE
- pine nuts
- sprigs of fresh rosemary

CONTINUED OVERLEAF

● Serves 12

UPSIDE-DOWN CHESTNUT AND PINE NUT PIE CONTINUED

Preheat the oven to 180°C/350°F/Gas Mark 4.

First make the 'topping'. Spread the chopped chestnuts over the base of a 25cm (10-inch) round cake tin. Add the pine nuts and soaked raisins and set aside.

Place all the caramel ingredients in a small saucepan. Bring to a boil over a medium–low heat, let it cook for approximately 10 minutes, then remove from the heat when the sugar has dissolved. Pour the caramel over the 'topping'.

Add all the dry pie ingredients to a large mixing bowl and combine. Blend all the wet pie ingredients in a high-speed blender until smooth then add to the mixing bowl with the dry ingredients. Combine together with a whisk until the mix is smooth.

Pour the mixture into the cake tin, making sure you cover the caramel mixture evenly. Bake for 1 hour, then remove from the oven and leave to cool. Flip the cake over so that the 'topping' is on the top. Decorate with pine nuts and sprigs of rosemary.

BEETROOT AND CABBAGE SAUERKRAUT

You can make numerous combinations of sauerkraut, so why not create your own version inspired by one of these recipes, yet adapted uniquely to you.

- –1 head of white cabbage
- –3 tsp salt
- –240ml (8fl oz/1 cup) beetroot juice

- –80ml (3fl oz/⅓ cup) apple juice
- –2 tbsp ginger juice

- –1 bay leaf
- –5 juniper berries

● **Makes 500g (1lb 2oz)**

Prepare your fermentation station well by wiping all the surfaces clean and sterilising the jars (or ceramic crocks) that you will use to store the prepared sauerkraut.

To sterilise your jars (or crock pots), bring a large saucepan of water to the boil, submerge the jars and boil for 10 minutes. Alternatively, heat up the oven to high, and place the jars (without any rubber or plastic parts) in the oven for 7–10 minutes.

Grate the white cabbage using a grater or slice thinly using a chef's knife. In a large mixing bowl, mix together the cabbage and salt and massage it with your hands for 5 minutes or until the cabbage starts feeling soft and slightly wilted. Add the rest of the ingredients and mix again for around 2 minutes.

Tightly stuff the sauerkraut into the sterilised jars (or crock pots), making sure that you press down well to release all the air bubbles and that all the vegetables are submerged under the water (kraut liquid) by at least 1.25cm (½ inch). If required, top up with extra water.

Loosely close the jar or cover it with a muslin (as the kraut will breathe). Leave on a kitchen counter at ambient temperature for 1–2 weeks, taste, and refrigerate when ready.

MACADAMIA FETA CHEESE

While we have been playing with plant-based cheese recipes for as long as we can remember, we feel that this recipe pretty much sums up our work in the nut cheese department. It provides everything you are looking for in a good, sophisticated cheese: texture, complexity of flavour, shape, colour and that unforgettable cheesy tanginess. It takes time to make, but if you are looking for a good autumn/winter kitchen project, it is so worth it. Perfect for a cheese board, as a luxurious present, on a cracker or mixed in a salad.

- 250g (9oz/2 cups) macadamia nuts
- up to 480ml (17fl oz/ 2 cups) water
- 1 probiotic capsule
- 120g (4oz/1½ cups) nutritional yeast
- 1 tsp salt
- 3ml lemon juice

● **Makes 3 cheese rounds**

Soak the macadamia nuts in plenty of water overnight. Drain and rinse well. Blend the macadamia nuts with 180ml (6fl oz/ ¾ cup) of water until smooth – add more water if needed to ensure smooth consistency. Add the probiotic capsule and blend again.

Place the mixture in a cheesecloth and tie it up. Put it in a sieve with a weight on top and let it drain and ferment overnight. The next day open the cheesecloth and add the nutritional yeast, salt and lemon juice and mix until it is well incorporated. Press the mixture down into 3 small cheese rings and leave in the freezer for 20 minutes.

Transfer the cheeses onto a dehydrator sheet and slowly remove the cheese rings. Dehydrate at 42°C/107°F for 36 hours, then flip around and dehydrate for another 36 hours, until the cheese starts crumbling but still retains its softness. Store in the fridge, in an airtight container.

PROVISIONS

WILD FOOD CAFÉ'S QUICK KIMCHEE

- 1 carrot
- 300g (10½oz) mooli
- 1 Chinese cabbage
- 2 probiotic capsules

SAUCE
- 20g (¾oz) spring onions
- 20g (¾oz) ginger
- 20g (¾oz) garlic
- 60ml (2¼fl oz/¼ cup) tamari

- ½ tbsp sunflower oil
- 2 tsp salt
- ½ tsp white pepper
- 60ml (2¼fl oz/¼ cup) water
- 1 tbsp chopped red pepper

● **Makes around 800g (1lb 12oz)**

Peel the carrot and mooli, cut them in half, thinly slice and add to a large bowl. Chop the Chinese cabbage into 1.25cm (½-inch) chunks and add to the bowl along with the powder from the probiotic capsules.

Place all the sauce ingredients in a high-speed blender and blend until roughly smooth. Add the sauce to the kimchee mix, massage thoroughly for around 5 minutes, transfer to an airtight container and leave at room temperature for 2 days.

WILD WISDOM

While the use of additional probiotics is unnecessary in wild fermentation, it does speed up the process and also ensures that the results are more consistent, especially if you have a varied temperature environment, which can affect the fermentation process.

BUCKWHEAT BREAD

This is an easy-going bread recipe that is versatile and always finds its place in our kitchen. Great toasted, as a side to soup and it also freezes well if you decide to make a bigger batch.

GLUTEN-FREE FLOUR MIX
- 180g (6½oz/1¼ cups) buckwheat flour
- 180g (6½oz /1½ cups) gluten-free plain flour
- 180g (6½oz /1½ cups) gluten-free bread flour

GLUTEN-FREE BREAD
- 600ml (1 pint/2½ cups) warm water (45°C/113°F)
- 1 tbsp agave syrup
- 2 tsp quick yeast
- 500g (1lb 2oz) gluten-free flour mix (see left)
- 2 tsp salt
- 1 tsp psyllium husk
- 50g (1¾oz/⅓ cup) flax seeds
- 2 tsp baking powder
- coconut or olive oil, to grease

Makes 1 loaf (12–14 slices)

To make the gluten-free flour mix, combine the flours and keep in an airtight container.

In a ceramic bowl, slowly combine 120ml (4fl oz/½ cup) of warm water with the agave and yeast, cover with a clean tea towel and let it sit for 10–15 minutes until the yeast becomes active.

In another bowl add the gluten-free flour mix, salt, psyllium husk, flax seeds and baking powder. Add the active yeast mixture and remaining warm water to the dry ingredient bowl and stir until well combined. Cover the bowl with a clean tea towel and let it sit for 30 minutes.

Preheat the oven to 200°C/400°F/Gas Mark 6.

Grease a loaf tin with oil and transfer the bread mix into it. Let it sit for another 15 minutes then bake in the preheated oven for 45–60 minutes.

PROVISIONS

RAW BUTTERNUT SQUASH BREAD

We feel enthused to create, explore and open up new frontiers of the bread tradition. You never know, this bread might be a life-changer for you! It is super-gentle on the body, yet extremely fulfilling. It keeps well in the freezer and can be toasted too.

- 300g (10½oz) butternut squash, cubed
- 210g (7½oz/2 cups) walnuts
- 2 pitted dates
- 1 tsp dried oregano
- 1 tsp salt
- 80g (2¾oz/1 cup) psyllium husk
- 55g (2oz/⅓ cup) flax seeds
- juice of 1 lime
- 120ml (4fl oz/½ cup) water
- olive oil, to grease

Makes 1 loaf (12–14 slices)

Blend the butternut squash in a food processor until you get small, fine pieces the size of a rice grain. Add the walnuts, dates, oregano and salt and blend again until you get a breadcrumb texture. Transfer to a bowl and add the psyllium husk, flax seeds, lime juice and the measured water. Mix everything with your hands until well combined.

Grease a loaf tin with olive oil and line with baking paper. Fill the tin with the bread mixture, pressing it down gently until it comes halfway up the tin. Make sure the mix is equally distributed. Dehydrate for 4 hours at 42–45°C (107–113°F). After 4 hours, turn the bread around and place it back in the dehydrator for another hour. The bread should have a crust but be slightly porous but moist throughout.

TOMATILLO SALSA VERDE

- 1 bunch of coriander, stalks removed
- 8 tomatillos
- 1–2 large spring onions
- ⅓ green chilli
- juice of 1 lime
- 2 tbsp extra virgin olive oil
- 1 tbsp apple cider vinegar
- pinch of salt
- pinch of freshly ground black pepper

● **Makes 500ml/ 18fl oz/2 cups**

Finely mince the coriander. Discard the outer lantern of the tomatillos and finely chop into small cubes (as small as it gets). Finely chop the spring onions and chilli.

Combine the coriander, tomatillos, spring onions, chilli, lime juice, olive oil and apple cider vinegar, sprinkle with salt and pepper and serve.

SOUR CREAM

- 1 slice of lemon with rind
- 2 tbsp sunflower seeds or sunflower butter
- 240ml (8fl oz/1 cup) water
- 2 tbsp apple cider vinegar
- 2 tbsp coconut cream
- 1 tbsp Tocos rice bran solubles (optional)
- ½ tsp salt
- 1 tbsp camu camu (optional)
- 2 tbsp olive oil

● **Makes 300ml/ 10fl oz/1½ cups**

To make the sour cream, place lemon and sunflower seeds or sunflower butter in a high-speed blender. Add just enough water to blend the seeds or butter into a completely smooth cream. Add the rest of the ingredients apart from the olive oil and blend again. Then fold in the olive oil gradually, while the blender is still blending on a low setting. Taste and adjust the flavours as required.

PUMPKIN SEED PATÉ

This recipe came about almost by accident as Joel was enthusiastically making a new version of a portable cheese to go onto our new pizza. We spent a day driving around with a jar of this 'cheese' in our car, and by the time we came back home and tasted it again, it had naturally fermented enough to closely match the flavours of a traditional paté, which Aiste couldn't be any happier about. This little number is an excellent source of protein (hello pumpkin seeds!), we love using it as a spread instead of hummus and as a base for salad dressings. It keeps well in the fridge, and is easy-going on digestion due to its probiotic content. Winner!

- 250g (9oz) raw pumpkin butter
- 260g (9¼oz) Tomatillo Salsa Verde (see page 127, or buy in store)
- 3 tbsp roasted pumpkin seed oil
- 3 tbsp olive oil
- 4 heaped tbsp nutritional yeast
- 1 tbsp salt
- 1 tbsp probiotic powder

● **Serves 2–4**

Mix all the ingredients together in a bowl, transfer to a clean jar and let it sit at room temperature for a day. Keep in the fridge.

SEAWEED TARTARE

We are absolutely in love with this simple, wild, mineral-rich recipe that wins over the hearts of seaweed lovers and haters alike. It is a perfect introductory dish to the vast world of seaweed, a wonderful accompaniment to any savoury meal, and goes so well with any autumn and winter recipe. So, make a big batch, store it in your fridge and mix it into your soups or stews, or add as a relish to any savoury dishes, especially roasted vegetables. This way you effortlessly add a portion of seaweed and raw, wild food – with its vast array of nutrients and trace minerals – to your regular food lifestyle.

- 150g (5½oz) mixed fresh seaweed (either wakame, nori, kombu, sea lettuce, dulse or a combination)
- 3–4 cloves of garlic
- 1 shallot
- 100g (3½oz/⅔ cup) gherkins
- 60g (2oz/⅓ cup) capers
- 60ml (2fl oz/¼ cup) apple cider vinegar
- 1 tbsp coconut palm sugar
- salt and pepper to taste
- 150ml (5fl oz/⅓ cup) olive oil

Makes ½ litre (18fl oz)

Rinse then soak the seaweeds in water for 10–15 minutes. Drain well.

Place the garlic and shallot in the food processor and mince. Add the rest of the ingredients apart from the olive oil and pulse until all the ingredients are well combined (while still maintaining a bit of chunk).

To emulsify the tartare, start to gradually pour the olive oil into the mix through the top, while the food processor is on. You can adjust to taste by adding more of any of the ingredients.

Store in a dry glass container with a layer of olive oil on top. Will last up to a month in the fridge.

PROVISIONS

SMOKY AUBERGINE SUNFLOWER SEED YOGHURT

With charred aubergines and raw probiotic sunflower seed yoghurt, for us this is a perfect, functional and smart fusion of raw and cooked food. It is fermented, so good for your gut health. It is protein rich from sunflower seeds, easy to digest due to probiotics.

- 140g (5oz/1 cup) sunflower seeds
- 1 aubergine (preferably white variety in season July–September)
- large pinch of salt
- juice of ½ lemon
- 2 tsp probiotic powder
- 5–6 tbsp olive oil
- ¼ small shallot, finely chopped
- ¼ tsp ground cumin
- ¼ tsp ground coriander seeds

Makes 250ml (8½fl oz)

Soak the sunflower seeds in water for 1–2 hours.

Make a few holes in the aubergine with a fork and grill it over the flame of a gas hob for 10–15 minutes or until the skin is charred and the inside is soft. Alternatively, bake in the oven at 200°C/400°F/Gas Mark 6 for about 20 minutes or until the inside is gooey and soft. Set aside on a few sheets of kitchen roll to cool and drain.

Drain the sunflower seeds, discard the water and blend the seeds in a high-speed blender with the salt and lemon juice and just enough water to form a smooth cream. Once you achieve a smooth and creamy consistency, remove from the blender and transfer to a glass jar. Mix in the probiotics, olive oil, shallot, cumin and coriander seeds.

Remove the aubergine flesh, discard the burnt skin (although you can leave in a few tiny pieces for an extra-smoky flavour). Chop the flesh as finely as you can – and mix into the sunflower cream. Adjust the flavour by adding more salt, lemon juice or olive oil. Close the lid and let it sit at room temperature for 12–14 hours then taste and refrigerate. It will keep refrigerated up to a week.

TERIYAKI CRUNCHY ALMONDS

There are a couple of snacks that always save our day when we are on the move and teriyaki crunchy almonds is one of them. The process of 'activation', or soaking the nuts to remove naturally occurring enzyme inhibitors, makes the almonds easier to digest; while the process of gently drying soaked almonds coated in an incredibly flavoursome sauce makes them so much crunchier and moreish. Wild alchemy in action.

- 400g (14oz/3 cups) almonds
- 3 tbsp chopped spring onions
- 2 tbsp olive oil
- 100g (3½oz) Teriyaki Sauce (see page 179)
- 1 tsp garlic powder
- 1 tsp onion powder
- 2 tbsp white sesame seeds
- 10g (¼oz) nori sheets

Serves 4–6

Soak the almonds overnight. Drain them, place on a dehydrator sheet and dehydrate at 45ºC/113ºF for 24 hours or until the almonds start becoming slightly crunchy.

After 24 hours mix the almonds with the rest of the ingredients except for the nori sheets and put back in the dehydrator for another 48 hours or until the almonds get dry and crunchy.

Cut the nori sheets into 1cm (½-inch) strips. Take the almonds out of the dehydrator and serve with some nori sheet strips.

BBQ COURGETTE FRIES

This is one of our favourite snacks to take on road trips, to the cinema or just to enjoy at home. We love to break up the pieces and scatter them over salads or eat alongside some heavenly creamy dip. So many variations and possibilities ... and a breath of fresh air after all the kale chips!

- 6 courgettes
- pinch of salt
- 80g (2¾oz/½ cup) naturally cured pitted black or pink olives

- 4 tbsp apple cider vinegar
- 4 tbsp lime juice
- 6 tbsp sunflower oil
- 6 tbsp tamari

- 6 tbsp coconut sugar
- 2 tsp smoked paprika
- 2 tsp ground cumin
- 2 tsp ground black pepper

Serves 2–4

Thinly slice the courgettes lengthwise using a mandolin. Place in a mixing bowl, sprinkle with salt and leave to soften while preparing the marinade.

Blend all the other ingredients in a high-speed blender. Drain all the excess water from the courgette then add to the sauce.

Lay out the courgetti strips on a dehydrator sheet and dehydrate at 45°C/113°F for 24 hours, or until fully dry and crispy. Store in an airtight container.

GROW

EARTH

ENVIRONMENT

Earth is the spirit of the North, which can be called upon (by facing this direction) to be still and crystallised, like ice formations. It is the coldest of winter, a time of incubation, as represented by nuts and seeds. It is the darkest midnight hours; our elder years, the wisdom of laughter and joy.

It is about the material manifestation of all physical forms: from the body, its health and its strength, to our mastery of physical resources, and the wisdom to be generous with these. It is grounding and moist in its essence and carries salty and umami flavour spectrum. In our bodies the element Earth is represented by our bones and physical structure. It is the mineral kingdom: from stones, to crystals, to mountains and valleys. On a symbolic level, the direction of the North and the element Earth is often represented by the buffalo (in particular white buffalo), deer and any kind of stones and crystals. In terms of incense and aroma, this direction is often associated with the rich smoke of amber, which is said to help us remember our roots, and in turn our essence. It is the new moon.

The season of winter and the element of Earth is here to remind us of the constant ebb and flow of life's cycles. That after the peak activity and recreation of summer and the harvest of autumn comes a time to rest, reflect, relax and mature; to concentrate and crystallise. Like a wild acorn, dormant during winter, element Earth is about all the ways to gather strength, structure and wisdom that will burst out with the first rays of light in spring. Naturally, it is an invitation to explore all the ways to nourish ourselves — internally and externally. Being in balance with the element of Earth brings us to the internalising practices and rituals of self-love and self-awareness to know what is good for us. We are invited to slow down and to master ourselves. It is a great time to really tune in to our bodies, to the crystalline structure of our bones, and to the sheer miraculous abundance of material existence.

RITUALS

GROUNDING AND FOREST BATHING

All the most inspiring humans in history have a very strong track record of spending time meditating and contemplating in nature. Not as a theory or an intellectual idea, but actively immersing themselves in the practice. Commit yourself to the quest of finding a tree or a patch of ground somewhere you feel calm and peaceful. It can be profoundly nourishing to turn this activity into a regular practice. It dissipates any build-up of mental, emotional, physical static and stress. The Earth is proven to be continuously radiating a field of free electrons – the ultimate antioxidant – so just plug in through the direct conductive contact of touch. Whenever you can, take your shoes off, connect to the natural currents of the Earth directly. This simple yet profound practice is extremely stabilising as it cools the fires of inflammation resulting from accumulated toxicity and stress. It purifies us with the steady frequencies of Earth's immovable essence: something that has been here before us and will be here long after us.

Our generation has increasingly become known as an indoor generation. This recent development in our evolution comes with many unexpected and sometimes unacknowledged side-effects, from compromised immune systems to mental health issues. So many of us, especially in urbanised settings, don't spend enough time outside. For us it has to be at least 1½–2 hours a day, not counting the times when we are in transit in a car or a bus. It is such simple common sense, yet so many of us have forgotten how to just be and relax in outdoor spaces.

Shinrin-yoku is a term that means 'forest bathing'; as a practice it was developed in Japan during the 1980s and has become a cornerstone of preventive health care in Japanese medicine. Researchers in Japan and South Korea have established a robust body of work on the health benefits of spending time immersed in a living forest.

The atmosphere of a forest is not only overflowing with electrifying oxygen, hydrogen and nitrogen, it is often drenched in an aroma from all of the plants that are transpiring vapours of living waters. It is full of life-giving antioxidants and highly charged substances, such as pine pollen, and medicinal mushroom spores. The vibrations, sounds and a fully immersive experience of forest bathing rebalances us unlike anything else, allowing stress and static to melt away. Our senses become nourished, tuned-in and relaxed. The harsh corners and flat surfaces of most human-built environments no longer confine our fullest expression. This facilitates the flow of our natural innate happiness and comes with the full spectrum of physical, mental, emotional and spiritual benefits. At least once a month, or as often as you need, take time to make a trip to a forest near you. Spend at least 2 hours, better still up to a day, hiking, moving or sitting, tuning in to the environment with your senses. Try just being in the forest alone, or with your loved ones, without a solid plan to follow.

MOVEMENT

We are so immeasurably blessed to have our bodies, as well as being able to move them. The unlimited freedom we have of putting on our favourite song out of all the music ever created is miraculous in itself, let alone the potential gift of being able to dance to it every day.

Nourish the soul and celebrate your bodies by playing music and 'sweating your prayers' with wild abandon. Move the body in each and every way you feel guided to, move the body with a wild abandon and flow, free of contractions and blockages.

To dive further, explore and immerse yourself in a holistic movement practice such as one of the many variations of hatha yoga, kundalini yoga, tai chi or martial arts. Whatever form of movement you practise remember to connect your breath with your movement and focus on the holistic alignment of body, mind and soul. This will make you immensely happy.

RECAPITULATION MEDITATION

Our favourite (and most potent) simple practice in preparation for conscious rest is a daily recapitulation meditation. You don't have to sit down in a meditation posture or to stop whatever you are doing, just allow some internal space to review your day combined with deep, free-flowing, full belly breaths.

Acknowledge all the people you met that day, all the places you spent time in. Focus and remember all the conversations you had, observe your thoughts, reactions and responses, without getting involved. It is a great way to review your day with a bit of distance, find some perspective and keep your memory in a great shape. It is almost like you

get to live each day twice (at least in your awareness). It is an excellent way to make sure that the days don't pass by like a conveyor belt of busy blurriness.

It is also an opportunity to reflect, acknowledge any mistakes and improve awareness for the following day creating resolution and reconciliation, giving a sense of calmness and closure for the night. Make sure your mind doesn't linger on anything that happened. It is time to let go, which will allow your rest to be deeper.

Different versions of this practice are echoed through many different traditions in the world, both ancient and modern, from India, China, Africa, and Australasia to South and North America. Integrate it as part of your evening rituals and practices in preparation for bedtime.

Wild practice: the art of unwinding

Keep the bed space free of all distractions, technology, phones and clutter. Use flowers, plants, crystals, natural incense and objects you found in nature or that are dear to you to create an environment that is conducive to deep relaxation. Leave at least two hours (preferably four) after eating solid food before you go to bed. Pay attention to your last meal of the day – it signals the beginning of a nightly fast. Whatever you choose to eat, make sure your final meal of the day is slow, mindful, and brings you back to the centre of yourself. This can hugely influence the quality of rest and even affect dreaming. The heavier the nighttime meal is, the bigger the likelihood of nightmares, as the body struggles to digest and obtain enough oxygen for both the stomach and the brain, let alone for all of the cells to come into the greatest holistic, cooperative homeostasis. Extend a similar approach to all technology, social media and media use in the evenings. Allow time for your mind to switch from an outward mode to an inward mode, be present with yourself and your loved ones, engage in creative and nourishing activities. Have a relaxing cup of your favourite nighttime drink, such as lavender or chamomile tea. Savour it, and as you do, go through a recapitulation meditation.

NOURISHING OUR BODIES FROM INSIDE OUT

Cleansing the toxins of our modern lifestyle, such as mercury and heavy metal residues in general, can dramatically change our state and the way we feel and function on a day-to-day basis. We love using clay and charcoal in food and beauty, as both are extremely porous and have massive surface areas, which act like sponges, especially when combined with the psyllium, absorbing and binding any toxicity and inorganic substances from the body.

◊ Wild practice: detoxifying and grounding bedtime drink

This is a great seasonal practice to enjoy in the evenings a couple of days a week over winter and early spring.

- 1 tsp food-grade clay
- 1 tsp food-grade charcoal
- 5g psyllium husks
- 500ml water

Put all the ingredients into a blender and blend lightly until just combined.

EDIBLES

The winter season, with its cold and short days and long dark evenings, calls for a deeper, more grounded nourishment. This time of the year — and correspondingly the last meal of the day — can be so rich with its offering. We find our earthy, wintry happiness in deep-hued life-affirming feasts. That doesn't mean that you should fill winter days with heavy meals — not at all! Rather, use it as a guidance tool to support yourself when you feel like you require earthiness and comfort in your life — be it winter, a cold summer's day, an occasion for a special meal or celebration, or any time when you would like to receive deeply rebuilding nourishment.

In the Wild Wellbeing Compass, North–Earth sits opposite the South–Fire, with its myriad spicy and sour flavours. Fats and spices are a match made in heaven: whenever there is too much of one, the other balances and neutralises the effect. Also, since some nutrients are only fat-soluble, adding a small quantity of high-quality-raw, unprocessed fat or oil into meals and drinks makes them more bioavailable. Many spices are naturally warming so it makes sense to place them as a central feature of wintertime cuisine. It is a perfect time for exploring the flavours and medicinal qualities of spices from near and far, in dishes such as fragrant broths, stews and curries to uplift our mood and strengthen and restore our bodies and immune systems.

It is also the time when we stock up on our favourite winter provisions. We make sure to have at least a few containers of our favourite varieties of olives — a naturally fatty, savoury food to snack on throughout the day. We stock up on local and European nuts such as hazelnut, cobnut, chestnut, almond, pine nut, pistachio and walnut. The oils within the nuts are incredibly delicate — they react to light and oxygen as soon as they are shelled — so we seek them out in their shells to really tap in to their full freshness, potency, flavour and medicinal power. It's also a great way to do a portion reality check: it's harder to overeat more than a handful of nuts in one go when shelling by hand and enjoying them fresh. We also make more soups, drink more herbal teas, cacao-based elixirs and other warm alchemical potions (see pages 53, 192 and 202).

WABI-SABI KALE SALAD

This salad is a wonderful addition to your 'raw-centric' winter repertoire, complete with warming kimchee, flavourful mushrooms and crunchy nuts. It is everything we like to eat in one bowl.

CARAMELISED STICKY MUSHROOMS
- 40g (1½oz) shiitake mushrooms
- 40g (1½oz) oyster mushrooms
- 2 spring onions, chopped
- 1 tsp white sesame seeds
- 2 tbsp Date Sauce (see page 179)
- 1 tbsp olive oil

SALAD
- 80g (2¾oz/generous 1 cup) destalked kale
- 120ml (4fl oz/½ cup) Sour Cream (see page 127)
- 1 tbsp hemp seeds
- 2 tbsp red pepper, diced
- 2 tbsp cucumber, diced
- 2 tbsp Wild Food Café's Quick Kimchee (see page 124)

- 2 tbsp Caramelised Sticky Mushrooms (see left)
- 1 tbsp wakame seaweed, soaked
- 2 tbsp boiled chestnuts

TO GARNISH
- spring onion
- sesame seeds
- avocado
- Teriyaki Crunchy Almonds (see page 131)

● **Serves 2**

To make the Caramelised Sticky Mushrooms, slice the shiitake mushrooms and shred the oyster mushrooms then add all the ingredients to a bowl and stir together. Spread out on a dehydrator sheet and dehydrate at 45°C/113°F for 3 hours. After 3 hours, flip around and dehydrate for another 3 hours or until the mushrooms are dry on the surface, but still soft and chewy.

To make the salad, wash and drain the kale then remove and discard the stalks. Add the kale to a bowl and massage well with your fingers until the kale starts to soften and wilt. Mix in the Sour Cream and hemp seeds and transfer to a serving bowl. Add the red pepper and cucumber around and on top of the kale. Add the kimchee, Caramelised Sticky Mushrooms, wakame and chestnuts. Garnish with spring onion, sesame seeds and Teriyaki Crunchy Almonds.

MAYAN SALAD

The Mayans revered cacao as their sacred medicine and the food of the gods. We also know that they never consumed cacao sweet, so this recipe with red quinoa and cacao nibs is an ode to a different kind of relationship with cacao and the times when it was revered as sacred.

- 4 tbsp red quinoa
- 6 pieces of tenderstem broccoli or purple sprouting broccoli
- juice of 1 lime
- 1 tbsp olive oil, plus extra to drizzle

- ½ tsp salt
- ½ head of Romanesco broccoli
- 40g (1½oz) Mustard Dressing (see below)
- 120g (4oz) mixed salad leaves

- 1 tbsp cacao nibs
- 2 tbsp pomegranate seeds
- 40g (1½oz) Smoky Coconut Chips (see page 182)
- 2 figs, halved or quartered
- ½ avocado, sliced

● **Serves 2**

MUSTARD DRESSING
- 125ml (4fl oz/½ cup) apple cider vinegar
- 3 tbsp wholegrain mustard
- 100g (3½oz/½ cup) coconut sugar
- 1 tbsp dried oregano
- 1 tsp black pepper
- pinch of salt
- 300ml olive oil

A day before preparing the salad, wash the quinoa thoroughly, place in a flat container and cover with a wet muslin. Twice a day, wet the muslin so that the quinoa stays wet. After 1 day, the quinoa will have sprouted. You can also choose to use cooked quinoa instead of sprouting it.

Thinly slice the tenderstem broccoli and marinate it for 2 hours in the lime juice, olive oil and salt. Gently blanch the Romanesco broccoli in boiling water.

To make the Mustard Dressing, mix all the dressing ingredients apart from the olive oil together in a bowl. Slowly whisk in the olive oil.

In a mixing bowl, place the salad leaves, quinoa and Mustard Dressing. Add the tenderstem broccoli and toss it with the dressing.

Divide the salad between 2 plates and sprinkle on the cacao nibs, pomegranate seeds, Smoky Coconut Chips, figs and avocado. Garnish with the Romanesco broccoli and a drizzle of olive oil.

WILD BURGER

There is something very special about the rich umami flavours of a burger pattie, the possibilities of creamy dips, sauces and pickles, the spectrum of flavours available to play with, and, of course, the bread that makes burgers one of the most popular foods in the world. Our commitment was to make the best burger in town – not just the best veggie burger, but a burger that everyone would enjoy eating regardless of their dietary preferences. It had to be meaty in flavour, texture and, most importantly, nutrition. We knew that the lentil and starchy-vegetable-stuffed burger patties were not satisfying enough for us or for anyone else. And so, we embarked on a journey to find the best burger ingredients and flavours.

PATTIE SAUCE
- 2 tsp olive oil
- 2g (scant ⅛oz) garlic
- 25g (1oz) pau d'arco powder (optional)
- ¼ lime (peeled, leaving the white pith)
- 1 tsp tamari
- ¾ tsp ground black pepper
- 3g (scant ⅛oz) smoked paprika
- 5g (⅛oz) brown miso

BURGER PATTIE
- 10g (¼oz) dulse
- 100g (3½oz) red pepper
- 80g (3oz) shiitake mushrooms
- 55g (1¾oz) butternut squash
- 25g (1oz) beetroot
- 40g (1½oz) red onion
- 25g (1oz/⅛ cup) naturally cured pitted black olives

- 175g (6¼oz/1⅛ cups) naturally cured pitted pink olives
- 50g (1¾oz/⅓ cup) sunflower seeds
- 45g (1½oz/¾ cup) parsley, finely chopped
- 20g (¾oz/⅛ cup) ground flax seeds
- 40g (1½oz/¼ cup) ground flax seeds, for coating

● **Serves 2–4**

First make the pattie sauce. Blend all the ingredients in a food processor until smooth but with a little bit of chunk left. Set aside.

Next make the pattie. Soak the dulse for 2 hours, then drain and roughly chop. In a food processor, individually pulse the following ingredients one at time until you get small chunks, then set aside: the red pepper, shiitake mushrooms, butternut squash, beetroot, red onion, black and pink olives. Blend the sunflower seeds until you get a fine powder. Add all the burger ingredients, except the

CONTINUED OVERLEAF

146

WILD BURGER CONTINUED

SEEDED BUN (MAKES 5 PORTIONS)
- 15g (½oz) shallot, diced
- 100g (3½oz) butternut squash, pureed
- 75g (2¾oz/½ cup) sunflower seeds
- 50g (1¾oz/⅓ cup) flax seeds

- 125g (4½oz/¾ cup) chia seeds
- 60g (2oz/¾ cup) gluten-free oats
- ½ tsp salt
- 50g (1¾oz/⅓ cup) pumpkin seeds
- 2 tbsp nutritional yeast

- 125g (4½oz/¾ cup) ground flax seeds
- 125ml (4fl oz/½ cup) water
- 5g (⅛oz/generous 1 tsp) maple syrup
- 40g (1½oz/3 tbsp) coconut oil
- 1 tsp baking powder

ground flax seeds for coating, to a bowl and mix in the pattie sauce. Weigh out roughly five 110g (3¾oz) burger patties.

Coat both sides of the patties with the ground flax seeds. Dehydrate at 45°C/113°F for 8 hours and then flip over and dehydrate for another 4 hours or until the patties start drying on the outside but still retain softness inside.

To make the seeded bun, sautée the diced shallots until they become soft, then transfer to a large mixing bowl. Add the rest of the ingredients to the mixing bowl and combine. Let it sit at room temperature for around 30 minutes. Preheat the oven to 180°C/350°F/Gas Mark 4.

Weigh out roughly five 150g (5½oz) balls of the bun mix and flatten them evenly into large pattie-size cutting rings. Bake in the oven for 20 minutes, then flip around and bake for another 20 minutes until they're golden brown. Leave to cool for 30 minutes or in the fridge overnight.

Serve the burgers with any/all of the following: seeded bun, avocado, Garlic Mayonnaise (see page 181), Red Pepper and Goji Berry Marinara (see page 178), Aubergine Yoghurt (see page 130), lettuce, gherkin and a side of baked sweet potatoes or squash.

WILD WISDOM

Olives are one of our staples and a favourite European food. Packed with good fats, an olive is basically the purest olive oil parcel you will ever find. Rich in alkalising trace minerals and a vast spectrum of savoury, umami, bitter and sour flavours, olives are absolute stars in our kitchen. We only buy high-quality unpasteurised olives from small local producers in Europe. Call us crazy (or olive connoisseurs), but we usually only buy unpitted olives … because they are fresher and taste so much better! Since the day we opened the Wild Food Café, our team must have pitted countless thousands of kilos of olives – that's our dedication to this humble savoury fruit. We are continuously searching, tasting, exploring and pitting olives. For fans of savoury breakfasts, we also love to add a few olives to our breakfast meal.

MINI RAW PIZZA SUPERSTARS

There are raw pizzas ... and there are raw pizzas! This one has won our hearts over the years as it has a simple enough base to house the intricate flavours of the toppings and really allow them to shine. It is a perfect interactive dish for entertaining bigger groups: we love placing all the toppings on a sharing table and allowing all the guests to assemble their own pizzas with the toppings of their choice.

- 200g (7oz/1⅓ cups) almonds
- 680g (1lb 9oz) cubed butternut squash
- 5g (⅛oz) garlic
- 8g (¼oz) basil

- 5g (⅛oz) dried oregano
- 1 tsp salt
- 40g (1½oz/⅓ cup) ground flax seeds

- Red Pepper and Goji Berry Marinara (see page 178)
- Ayurvedic Pesto (see page 177)

TOPPINGS OF CHOICE
- steamed tenderstem broccoli
- Caramelised Sticky Mushrooms (see page 142)
- naturally cured olives
- cubed avocado
- Macadamia Feta Cheese (see page 123)
- halved cherry tomatoes
- samphire
- rocket
- pine nut parmesan
- olive oil, to drizzle

● **Makes 10 portions**

To make the pizza base, blend the almonds in a food processor until a fine powder, transfer to a mixing bowl and set aside. Blend the butternut squash, garlic, basil, oregano and salt in a food processor until you get a fine purée. In a mixing bowl, mix the ground almonds, butternut squash purée and ground flax seeds until you get a nice doughy consistency.

Divide the mixture into 100g (3½oz) balls, thinly spread out 4 balls on each dehydrator sheet and dehydrate at 57°C/134°F for 4 hours. Turn over and dehydrate for another 2 hours or until the pizza bases are dry, but not yet crispy.

Spread Red Pepper and Goji Berry Marinara on top of each of the bases and dehydrate for another 30 minutes or until the marinara or pesto base starts drying.

To serve, place a few dollops of Ayurvedic Pesto on each base, add a selection of toppings of your choice and finally add a drizzle of olive oil.

151

RAW WILD CURRY

Using whole ground-up spices is an excellent way to give a unique character to any dish. Spices are medicinal powerhouses, and when used in a raw form they are even more active and medicinal. The tradition of Indian curry has been taken to a new direction here, combining the best of both worlds: raw and cooked. This recipe is a bit of an epic adventure. It takes time, playfulness and dedication to get to know the flavours and be able to balance them to suit your unique preferences. It is a great project for a slow, wintry weekend. Or, if you wish, make just one or two parts of the curry and use as sides with other dishes. Infinite possibilities.

ONION BHAJIS
- 10 shallots, thinly sliced
- 1 tbsp salt
- juice of 2 lemons
- 1 tbsp coriander, finely chopped
- 1 tbsp parsley, finely chopped
- 3½ bananas
- 1 tsp onion powder
- 2 cloves of garlic
- 1 tsp red chilli
- 4cm (1½-inch) piece of fresh root ginger
- 1 tbsp coconut sugar
- 1 tbsp fenugreek seeds
- ½ tbsp turmeric powder
- 50g (1¾oz/½ cup) coconut flour
- 100g (3½oz/¾ cup) ground flax seeds

● Serves 3–4

ONION BHAJIS
Prepare the bhajis the day before. To make the bhajis, place the sliced shallots in a large bowl and mix with the salt. Massage the shallots for 2–3 minutes until they release a liquid. Discard the liquid and add the lemon juice, parsley and coriander. In a high-speed blender, blend all the other bhaji ingredients apart from the coconut flour and flax seeds until smooth. Add the blended mix to the bowl with the shallots, add the coconut flour and flax seeds and mix everything together. Take a heaped tablespoon of the bhaji mix and place on a dehydrator sheet, making it flat and round. Repeat with the rest of the mix. Dehydrate the bhajis at 45°C/113°F for 6–8 hours or until they are almost dry but still slightly soft on the inside.

CONTINUED OVERLEAF

RAW WILD CURRY CONTINUED

CAULIFLOWER RICE
- 130g (4½oz) parsnip
- 200g (7oz) cauliflower
- 1 tbsp lemon juice
- ½ tsp salt
- pinch of saffron

YELLOW CURRY SAUCE
- 200g (7oz/⅔ cup) coconut cream
- 100g (3½oz/½ cup) coconut oil

- 2 shallots
- ½ tsp turmeric powder
- 2.5cm (1-inch) piece of fresh root ginger
- 2 cloves of garlic
- 2.5cm (1-inch) piece of red chilli
- 1 tbsp ground cumin
- 1 tbsp coriander seeds
- 1 tbsp fennel seeds
- 1 tbsp ground black pepper

- ½ tbsp fenugreek seeds
- 1 tsp ground cinnamon
- 1 tbsp salt
- 2 tbsp coconut sugar
- juice of 1 lemon
- juice of 1 lime
- 1 yellow pepper
- 1 red pepper
- 600g (1lb 5oz) pumpkin
- 150g (5½oz) sweet potato

CAULIFLOWER RICE

To make the cauliflower rice, pulse the parsnip and cauliflower in a food processor, making sure not to over-blend. Transfer to a bowl and mix with the lemon juice, salt and saffron. Set aside.

YELLOW CURRY SAUCE

To make the curry sauce, melt the coconut cream using a bain-marie or double-boiler until it becomes a creamy liquid. Add all the ingredients apart from the yellow and red pepper, pumpkin and sweet potato into a high-speed blender and blend until smooth. Transfer to a bowl and set aside. Place the yellow and red peppers, pumpkin and sweet potato in a high-speed blender and blend until very smooth using a tamper or pushstick. Add the other blended ingredients and blend together until the sauce warms up, reaching 42–45°C (107–113°F). Set aside.

GREEN CHUTNEY

To make the green chutney, blend all the chutney ingredients together in a high-speed blender or a food processor until smooth. Transfer to a bowl and store at room temperature.

GREEN CHUTNEY
- 100g (3½oz/3 cups) baby spinach
- 125g (4oz/2½ cups) coriander
- 125g (4oz/2 cups) parsley
- 1½ courgettes
- juice of 2 limes
- 1 clove of garlic
- 1.25cm (½-inch) piece of fresh root ginger
- 1 bunch of spring onions
- 1 green chilli
- 1½ avocados
- 1½ tsp nutritional yeast
- ½ tbsp ground coriander
- 1 cardamom pod
- 1½ tbsp salt

RED COLESLAW
- 100g (3½oz) beetroot
- 200g (7oz) red cabbage
- 125g (4oz) carrots
- 125g (4oz) parsnip
- 200g (7oz) celeriac
- 100g (3½oz) mooli
- 1½ tbsp finely chopped parsley
- ¾ tsp salt
- juice of ½ lemon
- 1½ tbsp olive oil

RED COLESLAW

To make the coleslaw, spiralise the beetroot, thinly slice the red cabbage and julienne or grate the carrots, parsnip, celeriac and mooli. Add all the coleslaw ingredients to a mixing bowl and massage them for 3–4 minutes, until the vegetables soften.

To serve, either place all the parts on a dining table in individual bowls for sharing or assemble individual portions with 1-2 serving spoons of each part present. Often during the colder season, we serve the curry with wild or black sprouted rice instead of cauliflower rice.

WILD WISDOM

When it comes to hardy vegetables such as sweet potato, pumpkin, carrot and squash, don't be afraid to blend them for a long time, until the purée heats up. The purée will naturally start heating up in a high-speed blender due to friction and might reach 50–70°C/122–158°F, going past the 'official' raw food guideline of 42–45°C/107–113°F. Ultimately, we find more benefits than drawbacks to this process, as it helps break down the cellulose and makes the raw vegetables easier to digest. It also ensures the smoothest possible result, texture-wise.

WILD MUSHROOMS ON TOAST

Wild mushrooms on toast happens to be one of our most loved staples in the autumn/ winter season. The flavour and vibration of the mushrooms connects us to the time of the year and speaks tales of the wild forest. We love how simple yet delicious this dish is, making it the perfect addition to your brunch repertoire.

- 2 tbsp sunflower or coconut oil
- 2 small shallots, finely chopped
- 3 cloves of garlic, minced
- 50g (2½oz) shiitake mushrooms, sliced
- 70g (2½oz) oyster mushrooms, shredded
- 50g (2½oz) wild chanterelles, shredded if large
- 4 tbsp white wine
- 4 tbsp water
- 140g (5oz/2 cups) kale, stalks removed
- 2 tbsp sweetcorn
- 2 tbsp cubed red pepper
- ½ tsp salt
- pinch of pepper

TO SERVE
- 2–4 slices of toasted Buckwheat Bread (see page 125)
- microgreens or fresh coriander

● **Serves 2**

Heat the oil in a frying pan over a medium heat then add the shallots and garlic and sauté until the shallots become translucent. Add the three kinds of mushrooms and cook for 2–3 minutes until the mushrooms soften. Add the white wine and water. After 30 seconds, add the kale, sweetcorn, red pepper, salt and pepper and toss.

Serve on top of 1 or 2 slices of toasted Buckwheat Bread and garnish with microgreens or fresh chopped coriander.

WILD WISDOM

You don't have to use wild mushrooms if they are not available, but whenever we can, we seek out wild ones and mix them into our regular cultivated mushroom mix.

CHICKPEA PANCAKES

It is worth celebrating life with pancakes from time to time. They are one of our favourite dishes for team breakfasts and we know that you will enjoy them as much as we do. Another brunch favourite, this version is super satiating. It is almost like a frittata and provides a lot of slow-release energy and protein from the chickpea flour.

- 115g (4oz) courgette, diced
- 115g (4oz) onion, finely chopped
- 200g (7oz/2 cups) chickpea flour
- 200ml (7fl oz/generous ¾ cup) water

- 2 tsp salt
- 1 tbsp baking powder
- 130g (4½oz) cooked red lentils
- 1 tsp turmeric powder
- 75g (2¾oz) sweet potato, finely chopped

- 2 tbsp finely chopped coriander
- 1 tsp chilli
- sunflower oil, to fry

TO SERVE
- Garlic Mayonnaise (see page 181)
- herbs of your choice

● Serves 7–8

Mix all the ingredients except for the sunflower oil together in a large bowl. Let it sit for 15–20 minutes.

Heat 1 tbsp of sunflower oil in a non-stick frying pan over a medium heat. Add 65g (2oz) of batter mix to the frying pan, gently shake the pan and let it cook for 2 minutes. Drizzle some oil on top of the pancake and flip and cook for another 2 minutes. Repeat with the rest of the mix.

Serve with Garlic Mayonnaise, or another dip of your choice, topped with some fresh green herbs.

MUSHROOM TIKKA SWEET POTATO

Joel: 'This dish was inspired by my grandma's home cooking from my childhood, namely her classic tikka masala chicken. When I managed to recreate the unique flavour of my grandma's cooking that was lingering in my memory, I shed a tear – it was so special. It just goes to show the power of connection and love that food carries.'

TIKKA SAUCE

- 60g (2oz/¼ cup) coconut oil
- ½ tsp salt
- 40ml (1½fl oz/scant 3 tbsp) lemon juice
- 5g (⅛oz) cumin seeds, freshly ground
- 5g (⅛oz) coriander seeds, freshly ground
- 5g (⅛oz) turmeric powder
- 2g (scant ⅛oz) freshly ground red chilli
- 5g (⅛oz) garlic powder
- 5g (⅛oz) onion powder
- 3g (⅛oz) ground ginger
- 7g (¼oz) garlic
- 50g (1¾oz) onion
- 7g (¼oz) fresh root ginger
- 5g (⅛oz) ground black pepper
- 75ml (3fl oz/⅓ cup) coconut water
- 60g (2oz) fresh coconut flesh
- 50g (1¾oz/generous ¼ cup) coconut sugar
- 75g (2¾oz) creamed coconut
- 7g (¼oz) miso
- 1 probiotic capsule

TO SERVE

- 2 sweet potatoes
- salt
- 200g (7oz) oyster mushrooms
- 240g (8½oz) Tikka Sauce (see above)
- olive oil, to drizzle
- microgreens, chopped chives, parsley or rocket

● **Serves 2**

To make the tikka sauce, blend all the ingredients in a high-speed blender until smooth and set aside.

Preheat the oven to 180°C/350°F/Gas Mark 4.

Wash and scrub the sweet potatoes, rub the skin with some salt and bake for 45–60 minutes. Once thoroughly cooked and soft, remove from the oven and allow to cool down for a few minutes. Shred the oyster mushrooms, and cook for a minute on each side in a very hot cooking pan. Transfer into a bowl and mix with the Tikka Sauce.

Cut the sweet potatoes in half lengthways, stuff with the mushroom tikka mix, drizzle with olive oil and top with freshly chopped herbs or microgreens.

WILD DOSA WITH SLOW-COOKED AUBERGINE

Our head chef, Thet, makes the best dosa. It is an excellent savoury brunch option, especially for slow weekends. Once you get this dish right – and it is easy – it will bring so much fun, variety and flavour into your kitchen, as with different toppings and fillings (raw and cooked) the possibilities are endless.

- 250g (9oz/1⅓ cups) urid dahl
- 250g (9oz/1⅓ cups) white quinoa

- 25g (1oz) shallots
- ½ tbsp salt
- 180ml (6fl oz/¾ cup) water

- 1 tsp baking powder
- sunflower oil, to grease

TO SERVE
- Slow-cooked Aubergine (see opposite)
- Sprouted Chickpea Hummus (see page 165)
- Mango and Fennel Chutney (see page 165)

● Serves 2–4

Start preparing the dosa mix two days in advance. Soak the urid dahl and quinoa in 2 litres (3½ pints/8 cups) of water overnight. Drain, wash the grain thoroughly and put it into a high-speed blender. Add the shallots and salt and 180ml (6fl oz/¾ cup) of water and blend until a smooth consistency. Add the baking powder and blend again. Transfer to a bowl, cover and let it sit at room temperature overnight.

Mix the batter well before cooking. Grease a pancake pan with a small amount of sunflower oil over a medium heat. Pour a large spoonful of the dosa mixture into the middle of the pan and slowly spread it in a circular motion. Let it cook for around 2 minutes, add a bit of oil on top of the dosa and turn it over to cook for another 20 seconds. Serve hot with Slow-cooked Aubergine, Sprouted Chickpea Hummus and Mango and Fennel Chutney.

SLOW-COOKED AUBERGINE

- 2 aubergines, cut in half lengthways
- salt, to sprinkle, plus a pinch
- 120ml (4fl oz/½ cup) sunflower oil
- 70g (2½oz) shallots, thinly sliced
- 20g (¾oz) garlic, minced
- 1 tsp paprika
- ½ tsp turmeric powder
- 720ml (1¼ pints/3 cups) water
- 1 tbsp tamari
- 5g (⅛oz) fresh coriander, chopped

Sprinkle the aubergine with salt to reduce its bitterness, then place vertically into a colander. Leave to drain for about 15 minutes.

Add the sunflower oil to a deep saucepan and heat over a medium heat. Add the shallots and sauté for 3–5 minutes, until they are soft and fragrant. Add the minced garlic and cook for another 2–3 minutes – be careful not to burn it. Add the paprika and turmeric powder and stir for around 20 seconds.

Place the aubergine in the pan with the flesh side touching the pan. Add a pinch of salt, the measured water and tamari. Cover the pan with a lid and let it cook for 15 minutes over a low heat. Flip the aubergine over, cover the pan again and cook for another 15 minutes. Turn the heat off and let it sit for around 15 more minutes. Sprinkle some fresh coriander on top and serve.

WILD WISDOM

The cooking times will depend on the size of the aubergine. It should be ready when the water evaporates – poke it with a fork to make sure it is silky soft throughout.

CONTINUED OVERLEAF

WILD DOSA WITH SLOW-COOKED
AUBERGINE CONTINUED

**SPROUTED CHICKPEA
HUMMUS**
- 350g (12oz) sprouted
  chickpeas, cooked
- 160ml (5½fl oz/⅔ cup)
  cooking water from the
  chickpeas
- 100ml (3½fl oz/scant ½ cup)
  extra virgin olive oil
- 2 tbsp lemon juice
- 30g (1½oz) tahini
- 5g (⅛oz) garlic
- ½ tsp salt

**MANGO AND FENNEL
CHUTNEY**
- 2 tbsp sunflower oil
- 55g (1¾oz) onion, chopped
- 5g (⅛oz) garlic, diced small
- 10g (¼oz) ginger, diced small
- 125g (4oz) fennel, thinly
  sliced
- 60g (2oz) mango, diced small
- 2 tbsp apple cider vinegar
- 1 tbsp agave
- 1 tsp salt

- 20g (¾oz) courgette,
  diced small
- 10g (¼oz) coriander,
  chopped
- 5g (⅛oz) mint, chopped
- 5g (⅛oz) parsley, chopped
- 5g (⅛oz) dill, chopped
- 2 tbsp extra virgin olive oil

SPROUTED CHICKPEA HUMMUS
To cook sprouted chickpeas, blanch for 5–7 minutes in boiling
water, drain and rinse. To make the hummus, blend all the
ingredients together in a high-speed blender until very smooth.

MANGO AND FENNEL CHUTNEY
Heat the sunflower oil in a saucepan over a medium heat.
Add the onion, garlic and ginger and fry for 5 minutes until they
turn slightly soft and fragrant. Add the fennel and cook for
5 minutes. Add the mango and cook for another 5 minutes,
then add the apple cider vinegar, agave and salt and stir well.
Add the courgette, then transfer to a mixing bowl and let it cool
down completely. Finally, add all the chopped herbs and extra
virgin olive oil to the bowl, combine, then serve.

WILD FOOD CAFÉ TEAM MEAL

While we are well known for our food, we are also famous for our team breakfast (or rather brunch) that happens every day, without fail, before we open our doors to the public. Team breakfast is an opportunity for us to come together as a family and explore new flavours. For the chefs it is an opportunity to share their work and recipes. It is often the space where new dishes emerge. They are different in character to our main menu items, designed to be made quickly, served in bulk, and provide plenty of sustenance for the day while delivering a serious portion of deliciousness to everyone involved.

- 125g (4oz) red onion
- 15g (½oz) garlic
- 1 green pepper
- 1 red pepper
- 1 yellow pepper
- 100g (3½oz) carrots
- 2 sweetcorn cobs
- 500g (1lb 2oz) tomatoes

- 60g (2oz) shiitake mushrooms
- 3 tbsp sunflower or coconut oil
- 1 tbsp tomato purée
- 240ml (8fl oz/1 cup) tomato passata
- ½ tbsp oregano
- 1 tbsp ground cumin

- 1 tsp cayenne pepper
- 1 tbsp ground coriander
- ½ tbsp cornflour
- 240ml (8fl oz/1 cup) water
- 200g (7oz) cooked red kidney beans, drained and rinsed
- 1½ tsp salt
- ½ tbsp chopped coriander

TO SERVE
- Serve hot with quinoa.
- Buckwheat Bread (see page 125) or Dosa (see page 162).

● Serves 4–6

Start the stew by finely chopping the onion and garlic, dice the rest of the vegetables and slice the mushrooms.

In a large saucepan, heat the oil over a medium heat. Sweat the onion and garlic until translucent. Add the diced vegetables along with the tomato purée and passata and let it cook for 2–3 minutes over a low heat. Add the oregano, ground cumin, cayenne pepper, ground coriander and the shiitake mushrooms. Let it cook for 5–10 minutes, until the vegetables are almost cooked through.

In a small bowl, mix the cornflour and water together. Add the kidney beans and half the cornflour mixture to the stew. Stir continuously as you add more of the cornflour and water mixture until the stew reaches a desired thickness. Add the salt and chopped coriander and taste.

LUSCIOUS LIVING LAKSA

Hint – the magic of this recipe is in the spices. Our wonderful head chef, Thet, masterfully combines the spices and herbs into a paste that will turn a fairly simple coconut broth into a luscious living laksa that you will always remember. This stuff is pure medicine.

LAKSA PASTE
- 400g (14oz) onion
- 50g (1¾oz) fresh root ginger
- 30g (1¼oz) galangal
- 150g (5½oz) lemongrass
- 3 lime leaves
- 80g (2¾oz) garlic
- 1 tbsp sweet paprika
- 1½ tbsp turmeric powder

BROTH
- 100g (3½oz/½ cup) coconut oil
- 8 curry leaves
- 1 cinnamon stick
- 375g (13oz) Laksa Paste (see left)
- ½ tsp ground cumin
- ½ tsp ground coriander
- 2 litres (3½ pints/8 cups) coconut milk
- 3 tbsp tamari
- ½ tbsp salt
- 1 litre (1¾ pints/4 cups) water
- 2 nori sheets

TO SERVE (PER PORTION)
- 200g (7oz) butternut squash
- 3 sugar snap peas, sliced lengthways
- 3 baby corns, sliced lengthways
- 50g (1¾oz) courgette noodles
- handful of bean sprouts
- 1 tbsp chopped coriander
- ½ tsp red chilli
- herbs or microgreens of your choice
- lime wedges

Blend all the Laksa Paste ingredients in a high-speed blender until you get a paste consistency. Set aside.

To make the broth, heat the coconut oil in a large saucepan over a medium heat. Sauté the curry leaves and cinnamon stick for 30 seconds to release the flavour, then add the Laksa Paste and cook for 10 minutes over a low heat while stirring from time to time. Add the ground cumin and coriander and cook for another 5 minutes, always stirring the mixture and being careful not to burn the spices. Add the coconut milk, tamari, salt and measured water and simmer for 45 minutes over a low heat. Toast the nori sheets in a dry frying pan and add to the laksa. Adjust the saltiness and flavour balance.

● Serves 6–8

To prepare the garnish, chop the butternut squash into small cubes and simmer in boiling water for around 2 minutes. Blanch the sugar snap peas and baby corn in boiling water for 30 seconds.

Serve the broth garnished with fresh courgette noodles, butternut squash cubes, sugar snap peas, baby corn, bean sprouts, red chilli and finely chopped fresh herbs or microgreens of your choice. Add lime wedges and a sprinkle of chopped nori sheets.

QUEEN OF THE FOREST

The idea for this dish came from our Brazilian sous chef, Guilli, who has a big smile and an even bigger heart. It reminded us that whenever we pour our heart into a dish, the results always exceed expectations. So, with some tweaks, this Brazilian plantain stew has been transformed into one of the star dishes for winter and always reminds us of our interconnected, global family. True nourishment for the soul on a plate.

- 100g (3½oz/½ cup) amaranth
- 200g (7oz/1 cup) black rice
- 1 tbsp hemp seeds
- 3g (⅛oz) spring onions, chopped
- 1 tsp salt
- oil, to fry

- 60g (2oz) red onion
- 70g (2½oz) red pepper
- 120g (4oz) plantain
- ¼ tsp camu camu powder
- 300ml (10fl oz/1¼ cups) canned coconut milk

- 50g (1¾oz) diced chow chow (optional)
- 150g (5½oz) diced tomatoes
- juice of 1 small lime
- 45g (1½oz/¼ cup) romanesco broccoli
- ½ tsp salt

TO SERVE
- 1 tbsp soaked wakame seaweed
- 4g (⅛oz/4 tbsp) coriander
- 2g (⅛oz) chopped spring onions
- pan-fried plantain
- 1 tbsp cacao nibs
- 1 tbsp hemp seeds

● **Serves 2**

Boil the amaranth in 400ml (13½fl oz/1⅔ cups) of water for 45 minutes over a medium–low heat, then drain. Meanwhile, cook the black rice in boiling water for 15 minutes, then rinse and drain. Mix the rice, amaranth, hemp seeds, spring onions and salt together in a large mixing bowl.

To make the stew, heat a little oil in a large saucepan and sauté the red onions until translucent. Dice 30g (1¼oz) of red pepper and 60g (2oz) of plantain and add it to the saucepan.

In a high-speed blender, blend the remaining red pepper and plantain, the camu camu powder, salt and coconut milk until smooth and add it to the saucepan. Put the lid on and let it boil for around 5 minutes, then add the chow chow, if using, tomatoes, salt and lime juice. Cook for another 5 minutes. Add the romanesco broccoli, put the lid on and cook for another 2 minutes.

To serve, divide the rice-amaranth mix between 2 bowls, serve the stew around the rice and garnish with wakame, coriander, spring onions, pan-fried plantain, cut lengthways, and cacao nibs.

171

NUT UNROAST

We love everything about this 'unroast' – including the fragrant cacao nibs. Every year at Christmas time we tweak it and adjust it slightly yet maintain the same hearty core. It is very fitting to have it as a main Christmas dish. Be daring and surprise your loved ones with something a little unusual and wild this year.

THE UNROAST
- 25g (1oz/¼ cup) pecans
- 25g (1oz/generous ¼ cup) macadamia nuts
- 25g (1oz/¼ cup) walnuts
- ½ tbsp miso paste
- 60ml (2fl oz/¼ cup) tamari
- 3 sage leaves
- 3g (⅛oz) garlic
- 50g (1¾oz/¼ cup) naturally cured pitted olives
- 40g (1½oz) fresh shiitake mushrooms
- 50g (1¾oz) parsnip
- 25g (1oz) Jerusalem artichoke
- 20g (¾oz) celery, chopped
- 12g (⅓oz) shallots, chopped
- 5g (⅛oz) leeks, chopped
- 8g (¼oz/1 tbsp) chia seeds
- 25g (1oz/¼ cup) gluten-free oats
- 25g (1oz/scant ¼ cup) cacao nibs
- 2½ tsp olive oil
- 12g (½oz/¼ cup) parsley

TO SERVE
- baby vegetables of your choice
- Roasted Vegetable and Madeira Wine Gravy (see page 180)

● **Serves 8–10**

To make the Unroast, put the pecans, macadamia nuts and walnuts into a food processor and pulse to crush, but be careful that it doesn't become too powdery. Put into a bowl and set aside.

Add the miso, tamari, sage, garlic and olives to the food processor and blend until you get a paste consistency. Put into a bowl and set aside. Add the mushrooms, parsnip, Jerusalem artichokes, celery, shallots and leeks to the food processor and pulse until you get chunky pieces. Transfer into a large bowl and mix with the crushed nuts, miso paste, chia seeds, oats, cacao nibs, olive oil and parsley and combine well.

CONTINUED OVERLEAF

NUT UNROAST CONTINUED

COCONUT BACON
- 200g (7oz/2½ cups) young coconut meat
- 3 tbsp BBQ Sauce (see page 176)

'TURKEY' MIX
- 60g (2oz) purple carrots
- 40g (1½oz) leeks
- ½ bunch of spring onions
- ½ tbsp rosemary
- 1½ tsp thyme
- 1 sage leaf
- 85g (3oz) cauliflower
- 800g (1lb 12oz) chestnuts
- 1 tsp nutmeg

- juice of 1 lemon
- 70g (2½oz/½ cup) naturally cured pitted green or pink olives
- 1 tbsp truffle oil
- 1 tsp orange zest
- 1 tsp chopped parsley
- 1 tsp salt
- 1 tsp ground black pepper

Take 100g (3½oz) of the mixture and press it into a 7cm (2¾-inch) cutting ring, then place on top of a dehydrator sheet. Repeat with the rest of the mixture. Remove the rings and dehydrate at 45°C/113°F for 4 hours. Flip around and dehydrate for another 4 hours or until it is dry on the outside but retains some softness inside.

COCONUT BACON
Meanwhile, make the Coconut Bacon. Slice the coconut meat into thin sheets. Mix the coconut sheets with the BBQ sauce and let it marinate for 3–4 hours. Place on a dehydrator sheet and dehydrate at 45°C/113°F for 90 minutes. Flip the sheets around and dehydrate for another 90 minutes or until the 'bacon' sheets are dry but not crispy.

TURKEY MIX

To make the Turkey Mix, pulse the purple carrots, leeks, spring onions, rosemary, thyme and sage in a food processor until you get a fine crumble. Transfer the mixture into a large mixing bowl and set aside. Add the cauliflower to the food processor and pulse until you get small crumbs. Add the cauliflower to the mixing bowl and set aside. Add the chestnuts to the food processor and blend until you almost get a purée. Add the chestnuts to the mixing bowl. Add the rest of the Turkey Mix ingredients to the mixing bowl, combine and set aside.

Take 50g (1¾oz) of the Turkey Mix and roll it into an egg-like shape. Repeat with the rest of the mix. Wrap it in Coconut Bacon and dehydrate at 45°C/113°F for 15–20 minutes.

Serve the unroast and coconut-wrapped 'turkey' with blanched baby vegetables of your choice along with a Roasted Vegetable and Madeira Wine Gravy.

BBQ SAUCE

Our go-to sauce for all things smoky and umami. This is an instant winner.

- 250g (9oz/1⅔ cups) naturally cured pitted olives
- 65ml (2½fl oz/¼ cup) apple cider vinegar
- 85ml (3fl oz/⅓ cup) lime juice
- 175ml (6fl oz/¾ cup) sunflower oil

- 185ml (6½fl oz/¾ cup) tamari
- 150g (5½oz/1⅛ cups) coconut sugar
- 15g (½oz/2 tbsp) smoked paprika

- 10g (¼oz/1½ tbsp) ground cumin
- 13g (½oz/2 tbsp) ground black pepper
- 3g (⅛oz) chilli

● **Makes 950ml (1¾ pints)**

Add all the ingredients to a high-speed blender and blend until you get a smooth texture. Transfer into a glass jar and store in the fridge for up to a week.

WASABI AIOLI

One of our favourite versions of a creamy, silky aioli – a handy mayo replacement for all kitchen situations: from salad dressings to spreads and dips. This is especially brilliant with sushi.

- 250g (9oz/2 cups) soaked cashew nuts
- juice of ½ lemon

- 2 tsp salt
- ⅛ tsp black salt
- 2 tsp maple syrup

- 140ml (4½fl oz/generous ½ cup) water
- 1 tsp wasabi paste
- 50ml (2fl oz/scant ¼ cup) olive oil

● **Makes 450ml (16fl oz)**

Blend all the ingredients except the olive oil in a high-speed blender until smooth. Once the sauce is smooth, pour in the olive oil very slowly and gradually, blending until the aioli emulsifies. Store in the fridge for up to 2 days.

AYURVEDIC PESTO

This pesto recipe was created by Joel with Pitta (Fire) body types in mind, who tend to overheat quickly and experience fiery emotions. The generally heating nuts are replaced with lighter and more cooling pumpkin seeds, and all the ingredients chosen, including the lime juice, have a cooling, calming quality. If you prefer to make a more warming (or your own unique) version of the pesto, feel free to replace the greens with greens of your choice, pumpkin seeds with nuts or seeds of your choice, and the sour element (lime juice) with either lemon juice or apple cider vinegar.

- 65g (2oz/1¼ cups) coriander
- 65g (2oz/1 cup) parsley
- 25g (1oz/1¼ cups) rocket
- 25g (1oz) dandelion
  or nettle

- 5g (⅛oz) garlic
- 5g (⅛oz) fresh root ginger
- 20g (¾oz/⅛ cup) pitted dates
- 70g (2½oz/½ cup)
  pumpkin seeds

- 1 tbsp nutritional yeast
- 5 tsp lime juice
- 65ml (2½fl oz/¼ cup) olive oil
- 35g (1¼oz) sea purslane
  or claytonia

● **Makes 400g (14oz)**

Add all the ingredients except the olive oil and sea purslane to a food processor and pulse gently until smooth. Do not over-blend the greens. Put the mixture into a bowl and mix the olive oil and sea purslane (or claytonia) into it by hand. Store in the fridge for up to 3 days.

WILD WISDOM

A recipe that combines fresh greens with a source of unprocessed fat (nut or seed) and seasoned roundly with plenty of lemony sourness (also broadly known as a pesto), is our favourite way of packing a lot of greens into our everyday food. Not only does this architecture of presenting greens taste amazing and is self-preserved by a high sour and oil content, the fat element of the recipe helps mellow down the bitter intensity of the fresh greens while helping extract the oil-soluble nutrients.

RED PEPPER AND GOJI BERRY MARINARA

There is such a massive discrepancy of flavour between local heirloom (or homegrown) tomatoes in summer and supermarket ones the rest of the year. For this reason, we created a marinara that features a close relative of the tomato – the red pepper – which is a lot more stable in flavour throughout the seasons.

- 500g (1lb 2oz) red pepper, chopped
- 90g (3oz) red onion, chopped
- 5g (⅛oz) garlic, chopped

- 7g (⅛oz) dates, pitted and chopped
- 3½ tsp lime juice
- 7g (¼oz) smoked paprika
- 1 tsp salt
- 25g (1oz/4 tbsp) goji berries

- 8g (¼oz) coconut sugar
- ½ tsp apple cider vinegar
- 5g (⅛oz) garlic
- 4g (⅛oz) thyme
- 4g (⅛oz) oregano

● **Makes 750ml (1¼ pints)**

Mix the red pepper, onion, garlic and dates with the lime juice, 3g (⅛oz) of the smoked paprika and the salt. Spread on a dehydrator sheet and dehydrate at 57°C/134°F for 4–5 hours or until soft and tender.

Soak the goji berries in warm water for around 15 minutes, then drain. Blend all the above in a high-speed blender with the rest of the ingredients until smooth. Store in the fridge for up to 5 days.

WILD WISDOM

Feel free to replace the red pepper with good-quality tomatoes when making this recipe in summer and early autumn. You can also use a probiotic capsule or add a tablespoon of unpasteurised miso to prolong the shelf life and increase the probiotic content.

DATE SAUCE FOR A GOOD SWEET 'N' SOUR MARINADE

This is a versatile savoury, sour, sweet and spicy marinade sauce perfect for myriad uses. We are certain it will come in handy in your kitchen creations.

- 85g (3oz/½ cup) chopped dates
- 180ml (6fl oz/¾ cup) tamari
- 80ml (3fl oz/⅓ cup) olive oil

- 110g (3¾oz/½ cup) coconut sugar
- 120ml (4fl oz/½ cup) water
- ½ tbsp garlic powder

- ½ tbsp onion powder
- 60ml (2½fl oz/¼ cup) apple cider vinegar
- ½ tbsp ground black pepper

● **Makes 550ml (19fl oz)**

Blend all the ingredients in a high-speed blender until smooth. If you find the consistency to be too thick, add a little bit of water and blend again. Store in the fridge for up to a week.

TERIYAKI SAUCE

This is one of our favourite marinades to coat any vegetable, nut, seed or mushroom with prior to dehydrating or roasting. It adds so much flavour.

- 80g (3oz/½ cup) dried apricots
- 120ml (4fl oz/½ cup) tamari
- 120ml (4fl oz/½ cup) rice mirin

- 1 small clove of garlic
- 160g (5¾oz/½ cup) maple syrup
- 60ml (2fl oz/¼ cup) apple cider vinegar

- 100g (3½oz) brown miso
- 120ml (4fl oz/½ cup) water

● **Makes 250ml (8½fl oz)**

Blend all the ingredients in a high-speed blender until smooth. You might need to add some more water if the sauce is too thick. Store in the fridge for up to a week.

ROASTED VEGETABLE AND MADEIRA WINE GRAVY

Perfect for Christmas and all occasions deeply wintry and social.

- 30g (1¼oz) leeks
- 1 clove of garlic
- 75g (2¾oz) chestnut mushrooms
- 75g (2¾oz) beetroot
- 30g (1¼oz) celery

- 75g (2¾oz) carrot
- 55g (1¾oz) cauliflower
- 60g (2oz) onion
- 110g (3¾oz) aubergine
- 1½ tbsp olive oil
- 50g (1¾oz /¼ cup) tomato purée

- 5g (⅛oz) kombu
- 1.25 litres (2 pints/5¼ cups) water, plus 2 tbsp
- 240ml (8fl oz/1 cup) Madeira wine
- ½ tbsp cornflour

● **Makes 750ml (1¼ pints)**

Preheat the oven to 200°C/400°F/Gas Mark 6.

Thinly slice all the vegetables and place them in a deep roasting tray. Drizzle over the olive oil, add the tomato purée and kombu and mix well. Roast in the oven for approximately 90 minutes, checking and flipping around every 30 minutes until all the vegetables get crispy and brown.

Transfer the vegetables into a large saucepan and add 1.25 litres (2 pints/5¼ cups) of water and the Madeira wine and boil at a high heat until it has reduced by half. Strain the liquid into another saucepan.

Mix the 2 tbsp of water and the cornflour in a cup until well combined. Slowly add the cornflour and water mixture into the gravy pan and whisk together until well combined – it has to become thicker. Adjust saltiness to taste.

GARLIC MAYONNAISE

So versatile and amazing, it is basically everyone's favourite dip.

- 10g (¼oz) dry wakame seaweed
- 200g (7oz/2½ cups) coconut meat
- 14g (½oz) garlic

- 5 tsp agave nectar
- 5 tsp lemon juice
- 1½ tsp apple cider vinegar
- ½ tsp salt
- 75ml (3fl oz/⅓ cup) water

- 100ml (3½fl oz/scant ½ cup) olive oil
- 5g (⅛oz) dill
- 10g (¼oz/1¼ tbsp) capers

● **Makes 250ml (8½fl oz)**

Soak the wakame for 10 minutes, drain and rinse. In a high-speed blender add the coconut meat, garlic, agave nectar, lemon juice, apple cider vinegar, salt and water and blend until smooth. While the blender is still going on a medium speed, slowly and gradually fold in the olive oil.

Once the mixture has emulsified, transfer it to a container. Finely chop the dill, capers and wakame and mix it into the sauce with a wooden spoon. Store in the fridge for up to 3 days.

TOMATO SALSA

A good tomato salsa is one of the simplest yet most sophisticated dishes that can completely transform any meal, or even proudly take a central role on a plate. This is especially good when tomatoes are in their peak season, ripe and filled with the sweetness of sunshine.

- 600g (1lb 5oz) heritage tomatoes
- 75g (2¾oz) shallots
- 10g (¼oz) coriander, chopped
- 10g (¼oz) parsley, chopped
- ½ tbsp olive oil
- 1 tbsp lime juice
- ½ tsp salt

● **Makes 700g (1lb 10oz)**

Deseed and cut the tomatoes and shallots into small dice. Mix all the ingredients together until combined. Store in the fridge for up to 3 days.

SMOKY COCONUT CHIPS

A versatile sprinkle with a power to uplift, transform and bring a creative delight to any dish – sweet or savoury.

- ½ tbsp organic smoked liquid
- 160g (5¾oz/½ cup) maple syrup
- 200g (7oz/2⅔ cups) coconut flakes
- 1 tsp salt

● **Serves 2–4**

In a mixing bowl, mix all the ingredients together. Transfer to a dehydrator sheet and dehydrate at 45°C/113°F for 24–48 hours, keeping an eye on them until they're crispy and fully dry. Store in an airtight container for up to a month.

HEART
OF THE
COSMOS

ENVIRONMENT

How do we reconcile all the complexities and paradoxes that come with our modern lives? How do we negotiate our apparent disconnection from nature and the bigger web of life, with an undeniable wild essence at the core of our beings that remembers and knows that we are, in fact, an innate part of this intricate cosmic dance? We start by filling in any missing pieces, and replenishing our cosmic connections.

There is an undeniable connection between us and the cosmos, both macro and micro. Nourishing and acknowledging this connection in our daily lives uplifts our spirit, helps us see the magic in everyday life, expands our perception of the bigger picture, connects us to inner peace and provides an immense sense of fulfilment and wholeness. Replenish this connection by curating an elevated space for self-care rituals and gathering items that feel sacred and special to you: symbols of different traditions, books and visuals from astronomy and astrology, representation of stars, sacred geometry and various portrayals of spirit that are in tune with your world view.

RITUALS

LIFE AS CEREMONY

Use the timeless art of intentional ritual to
rekindle the knowing that everything can
be celebrated and made sacred, meaningful
and interconnected through the alchemy of
our appreciation, perception and presence.
Create a ritual space wherever you are: either
in the office, at home or in nature. Navigate
your vibrational tone (mood) and cuisine with
subtle, less dense tools such as essential oils,
botanical essences, herbal infusions, positive
reminders and sacred sound. Remember to
regularly create and curate spaces that have a
sacred quality to them. Practise the alchemical
art of building an altar. Place things that are
important, unique and symbolic to you to
honour all aspects of your life. Celebrate your
connection to the cosmos and the stars by
following the key astrological happenings of
the cyclical year. Use crystals, living plants and
natural objects you found in nature: feathers,
pine cones, fruit, candles, spices, resins, oils
and perfumes; images which are special to
you in relation to the element and time of
the year. Write a declaration from your heart,
and place it on the altar. Remind yourself of
the seasonal foods and write down the ones
you are most eagerly looking to introduce to
your kitchen.

Regardless of which element the altar is
dominant in, we like to make sure that all four
elements are present for balance (feathers,
incense or burning resins representing air;
candle for the fire; a vessel of water for water;
crystals and rocks representing the earth).

While the practice of making an
altar is very potent and therapeutic
(especially when you take time to meditate in
front of it), you can transform it into a doodle
in your notebook, or just keep a series of notes
for that season. Whatever form it takes, make
a corner in your life to acknowledge each
element and each season. Study it and tune in
to it so you can notice and become more aware
each time the cycle comes around.

Wild practice: create a ceremonial space

Prepare and clear the environment with
a smudging herb of your choice (sage,
frankincense, juniper, palo santo, amber,
etc) or a natural incense stick. Turn off your
phone and leave behind your other immediate
activities, the thoughts and stresses of
everyday life. Allow yourself to tune in to
the present moment with the aid of a few
deep long breaths and/or a gong, chime,
bell, rattle, drum, flute or a singing bowl.
Whenever we gather in a ceremonial way, we
remind ourselves and others of the presence
of the four directions – the core of the wild
wellbeing compass – and acknowledge
that the elements are always within and
surrounding us.

Whether alone or in a group, gather
together into the centre of the space, the
centre of the heart. Mentally acknowledge
and give gratitude to all the elements and
circumstances that brought you to this
place here and now. Speak your intention,
out loud or in silence. When alone, utilise
the ceremonial space to engage in creative
activities, meditative contemplation, self-care

practices or journaling; when with company, engage in conducive, conscious sharing and conversations, mindful movement and dancing. While the deliberate intention is focused on the sacred, preserve the space by reserving all the ordinary chit-chat for later. To close the ceremony, smudge the space once again, give thanks to your experience and take a few moments of stillness to feel the rippling presence of peace within your heart and mind and extend it in gratitude to all your relations.

MEDITATION
Stillness is effortless.

Meditation means being present to the uniqueness of life in this very moment, to be fully awake on all levels. It is naturally accompanied with a soft effortless smile and the glow of inner peace, which occurs when we deliberately relax all of our muscles, and any areas of tightness and resistance. All meditation means is reconnecting to our inner awareness, our whole self, our inner nature, the balance at the centre of our compass. Most meditation practices focus on the breath, calming down, witnessing and watching the thoughts. We focus on a point where our inner vision meets our outer vision, our eyelids are fully relaxed. This naturally opens us into the space, which bridges our inner and outer worlds and brings us to the point of radiant awareness of ourselves, beyond the limitations of our daily lives.

Meditation can also be with us through all our daily activities – walking, running, dancing, doing yoga, talking to friends and working, reading a book, creating art, or having a cup of tea. When done with mindfulness, these activities can centre us and create spaciousness in our inner experience. Having inner spaciousness means we have more opportunity and time to respond to life and to ourselves with more deliberate awareness. This facilitates more openness to the flow of nourishment, more opportunity to offer the best version of our whole selves to the world. We balance the activity of our lives through moments of introspection, and whichever way we make it happen becomes our meditation.

Wild practice: a meditation practice

To start the day, spend 5–20 minutes sitting in your space inviting each and every one of your muscles to relax, eyes closed, focusing on your breath, experiencing the silence deep within and appreciating the rhythm of stillness.

APPRAYERCIATION

Illuminate your mind through counting your blessings: we playfully call this 'apprayerciation', or enthusiastically affirming that which feels fulfilling to us. Write three pages of aspects you appreciate about yourself, the people and things that inspire you and the experiences you look forward to. Keep writing in ways that make you feel expansive, open and inspired. Expand your perception and experience of who you are. No matter how challenging current life circumstances may be, we all have the unlimited capacity to build our momentum by finding things to appreciate and be grateful for. All thriving people start their day with at least some form of gratitude practice. Find your unique way of speaking your gratitude and appreciation to yourself and the world, and watch the magic unfold. Happiness and a sense of connection are a direct result of our practised ability to appreciate.

EDIBLES

Cacao is widely considered to be one of the most mystical foods. In essence, it embodies beautifully the vibration of the connection between the heart and the mind, between the ordinary and the mystical, between us and the cosmos, reminding us of natural connections that have always been here. It is intrinsically a wild food, deeply connected to the vibration of the forest – it's no coincidence that cacao is traditionally given as an offering in all occasions and ceremonies of love, from birthdays to Valentine's to Christmas and Easter. Due to its adulteration over the years, resulting in products that are high in refined sugar and processed dairy, not to mention the part that slavery (in cacao and sugar plantations) has played in its history, it has become entangled with the conflicting emotions of guilt and shame. But at its heart, we all know that chocolate symbolises joy, abundance, love, happiness, celebration and playfulness.

Cacao was so prized in the ancient American lands that it was chosen as the organic and edible currency of the Aztecs and Mayas, which due to its living yet perishable nature could not be hoarded. It contains well over 1,500 phytochemical constituents, of which some of the most well-researched compounds include anandamide, earning the name from the yogic word 'ananda', meaning bliss. Theobromine is the main medicinal alkaloid, which takes its name from the Latin *theobroma cacao*, meaning 'food of the gods'. Cacao gives energy, strength and is deeply nourishing for the cardiovascular, glandular and nervous systems. It is very rich in magnesium and trace minerals and also acts as a natural relaxant.

For the ultimate experience, quality, and to ensure that the cacao you are receiving has been produced with respect and reverence to the environment, it is important to obtain cacao from trusted reputable sources, preferably single-origin, Fairtrade, organic or in direct contact to growers to ensure that the transaction of this sacred food is clean in all aspects of the word. Traditionally the Mayans make a ceremonial cacao drink using just freshly ground cacao paste and water. It is a beautiful way to get to know cacao better in a ceremonial setting. In addition, we have given you a recipe that we use for special occasions. Make it and enjoy an evening of contemplation and creativity by yourself or with your loved ones, alongside a ceremonial space practice (see page 188). Cacao is very conducive to arts, crafts, writing, meditation, contemplation, singing and dancing and other forms of bodywork and movement.

CEREMONIAL CACAO

Share the cacao, clarify your intention and drink in total presence, appreciating and noticing all the flavour complexities. Revel in the effects and focus on connecting with and expanding the tangible feeling experience of your own inner glow, channelling it to relax each part of your body, and then towards the subject and object of your intended expression.

- 420g (15oz) cacao paste (the higher-grade the better)
- 1.5 litres (2¾ pints) of water or Invincibilitea or any herbal tea (see page 202) warmed
- 100g (3½oz) healthy fat source (fresh nuts/seeds, coconut milk, nut butter)
- pinch of salt
- 2 tsp vanilla extract
- ½ cup of dates
- ¼ cup of maple syrup

● **Serves 4–6**

Use a sturdy chef's knife to flake the cacao paste or chop it into small-enough pieces to fit in a blender. Warm the water to about 60C/140°F.

In a blender add the pieces/flakes of the cacao paste, and just enough warmed water or tea to cover all the ingredients. Blend well, until the cacao paste is smooth and well incorporated. Then add your choice of healthy fat source, dates and maple syrup and the rest of the warmed water or tea. Blend again, adjust the sweetness as required. Serve with a pinch of cayenne pepper if desired.

HEART

OF THE

EARTH

ENVIRONMENT

To heal the environment,
you must first heal
the environmentalist.

TICH NHAT HANH

At the heart of life on Mother Earth there
is a group of archetypal activities that are
universally practised and appreciated. All
the healthiest cultures around the world
participate in these regularly. They include
taking care of children, animals and plants;
gardening in synergy with nature; singing
and dancing; connecting to the environment
and each other through the seasons; creatively

living and celebrating life as art, ceremony
and ritual; making and sharing food; creating
and sustaining communities.

We are all indigenous, carrying an incredible
richness of the cultural melting pot that
is Mother Earth inside our bodies and our
cellular and genetic memory. Getting to
know more about our indigenous lineages
and traditional wisdom traditions is deeply
nourishing for our wild roots; it stimulates our
shared memory and brings out a natural sense
of acknowledgement, respect and humility.

RITUALS

EMPOWER YOURSELF WITH THE SEASONS

Each culture of the world carries its own tradition of celebrating and acknowledging the key turning points of the year and season: spring equinox and autumn equinox (when the day and the night are equal in length), summer solstice (when the day is the longest and the night the shortest) and winter solstice (when the night is the longest and the day is the shortest) in the Northern hemisphere. These are the pivotal points in our personal and collective rhythm. There is a moment of stillness and awe, a moment full of possibilities, an energetic burst as each season turns and transforms into another. Use this time to reset your body and your lifestyle to allow it to naturally attune to the seasonal changes that are taking place. Take a week or two each season to do a mini holistic cleanse, letting go of the former, reset, recreate and rebuild with the current new freshness. Feel nature's elements guiding you, inside and out.

Wild practice: connecting to the inner compass – daily alignment

Stand firmly, with feet shoulders-width apart, knees soft, tailbone lightly tucked in. Imagine an energetic cord pulling straight up your spine and out the top of your head towards the heart of the heavens, and the other end grounding you firmly to the heart of the Earth. Find your centre of stillness, become the bridge between the Earth and the sky. Connect with your breath, and with full presence, gradually turn in a circle, pausing to close your eyes in each direction, and noticing the difference in the felt quality of each direction. While facing East, connect yourself with the element of air by taking few deep conscious breaths and focusing on your body being filled with air, breathing not just with the lungs, but with every pore and cell. While facing the South, connect yourself to the beat of your heart and the warmth of your body, the pulsating and rhythmic fire. While facing the West, connect yourself with the element of water by feeling the waters of your body within you; by emotionally connecting yourselves to all waters of the world or taking a few conscious sips of water and setting your intention. While facing the North, connect to the element of earth, feel the structure and strength in your bones and in your body, feel the ground holding and supporting you from below. While facing the skies, connect to the heart of the cosmos and feel the transcendence and connectivity of all life. While facing the planet Earth, feel the heart of Mother Earth and the unconditional love, nature, food, shelter, wisdom and continuous support that she provides. While facing your own heart, your centre of centres, connect to the heart of all beings, the whole of humanity—past, present and future—converging here and now, and feel the connecting threads, the unity in diversity of all peoples. This practice can focus on whichever aspect of life's cycle you wish to amplify.

Wild practice: connecting to the inner compass – seasonal alignment

At the brink of each season, for a period of one to two weeks, reduce or completely eliminate caffeine from coffee and tea. Reduce or eliminate any other stimulants. These stimulants blur and distort our connection to the natural rhythms of our bodies, and often insulate and separate us from the connection to the bigger rhythm of the wild and the cosmos. Reduce or eliminate alcohol, fizzy drinks (including kombucha), fried, sugary, starchy staple foods and highly salted foods. Focus on eating simple whole foods and as few processed foods as possible. Follow with the same practice in other areas of your life. Reduce the daily distractions of the mind – from social media to conventional media; focus on being present with your life and relationships, refresh your meditation and movement practice, refresh your creative practices and crafts, even if it is just for 20 minutes each day, and spend time in nature, daily if possible. Combine, compound and stack the odds in favour of your wild nature: dare to exercise (alone or with a buddy) outside in nature and finish by foraging even a few edible leaves that you know very well. Reconnect with the elements of air, fire, water and earth in your own unique ways. Create an altar to signify and celebrate the seasonal changes in your life, creating intentions for your dreams and points of focus. Use the energy burst that inevitably comes with every shift of the seasons to honour and propel yourself in a direction of more wholeness and more thriving. Most of the time, all we need to do is to make space for it in our daily lives.

FLOWER MEDICINE: THE ESSENCE FOR THE SOUL

The Buddha famously gave the flower sermon once, where he did not talk for the whole discourse but simply held up a flower. Appreciating and feeling the beauty of a flower connects us to the beauty within us.

The geometry, harmony, beauty, colour, fragrance of a flower, not to mention its potency and fertility to perpetuate the beauty of planet Earth is easily taken for granted.

We are all surrounded by flowers all the time and can be uplifted by their presence if we allow it. In a vast array of ancient medicinal systems of the world, flowers are revered as the highest vibrational expression of the entire plant kingdom. It is a symbol of the soul and the spirit. Use it to refresh and bless yourself. Give an offering to someone of a pot of flowers or treat your altar to a bunch of flowers for when you are feeling heavy and burdened by everyday life.

🌍 Wild practice: bring flowers into your life

Make a commitment to drink 2–4 cups of flower infusions such as linden blossom, hawthorn flower, elderflower, lavender, chamomile and wild rose to nourish and uplift you for 30–100 days. Use a natural flower spray, flower essences or a flower bath, bring flowers back into your everyday life on a regular basis and be uplifted by connection with the high-vibrational essence of the plant world. Be sure that the flowers you choose for internal use are always neutral in their properties.

GROW A GARDEN

One of the best ways to enjoy a beautiful day on planet Earth is to participate in the profusion of life happening in a functional, flowering, fruitful garden with our nearest and dearest. A garden is the ultimate living altar of our lives. All life comes from the soil and all life returns to the soil. By participating in a simple act of tending to a plant – be it a jar of sprouts on our windowsill, some aromatic herbs, a fully established garden or allotment, or our favourite succulents — we get to connect with the living biology of the Earth (of which we are all an interconnected part) on a regular basis and rekindle the spark of our natural inner gardener. This is one of the simplest and most profound things we can actually have the power and responsibility over in terms of influencing ecology and our environment.

When we plant trees, gardens and forests we restore and practise appreciating more of nature's intricate living perfection. Make it easy for yourself by starting small, keep growing and see where it takes you. This practice comes with a rewarding sense of belonging, connection and fulfilment, and let's not forget all of the most delicious edible fruition you, your family and friends (human, furry and feathered) can feast on.

EDIBLES

Edible wild plants, sometimes derogatorily called weeds, are some of our greatest allies. These plants, with which we have the most ancient relationships, grow abundantly and freely with vigour, majesty and self-sovereignty. These are characteristics which, it is pretty much safe to say, all of us would truly choose to embody. In order to experience more of our whole selves it is good to follow the universally understood principle that we are what we eat. So it behoves us to reacquaint ourselves with these plant allies, and allow them to remind us of the wisdom of the Earth. Wild foods are genetically intact (not manipulated by man) and thrive in the wilderness without any help. They often contain a wide array of nutrients that are simply devoid in the modern diet. These nutrients help to maintain a holistic, long-term health and play a vital role in longevity and vitality.

Biodiverse natural environments, where wild foods come from, inherently regenerate without depletion and all aspects of these ecosystems are kept within balance. When we live and eat more in this way and incorporate more of these food groups into our lifestyle, our lives inevitably become more invigorating and invincible rather than bland and lethargic. All our cells are electrified and toned with the life force, trace minerals and electromagnetic field of these plants.

Mastering the art of making teas with edible local wild foods, sometimes called 'tonic herbs', and knowing that you can make a bountiful selection of wild herbal teas is invaluable to say the least. They can also serve as bases for smoothies, soups, sauces and dressings and are at the heart of the wild kitchen alchemy. It is an incredible alchemical practice that continuously encourages us to study, experiment and discover more of Earth's greatest gifts growing under our noses. Simply get educated and be wildly empowered. Especially in colder months, when nourishment requirements for our bodies increase, we like to have sufficient quantities of nourishing wild herbal tea – essentially made from the most commonly known wild foods – prepared in advance for whenever we feel like it.

In this section we solely showcase the herbs that are generic tonics (aka non-specific and act on multiple parts of the body at the same time). They bring nutritive strength and balance (raise what is low and lower what is in excess). They literally help the body to adapt, adjust and recalibrate itself depending on our emotional, energetic and physical surroundings. So, for example, they can help calm in times of stress. They can bring peace to a racing mind in the middle of the night. They can facilitate clarity when everything around feels in turmoil. They can give energy when we are tired. And even though for general safety it is advisable to take intermittent breaks from taking tonic herbal supplements, all the herbs and spices listed here are very basic and come with no side-effects.

WILD INVINCIBILITEA

Start by using herbs and spices you are already very familiar with. Find them in a local organic herbalist store, online or, if your circumstances allow, forage for them in your local wild environment. If you are not familiar with the herbs and spices and their effects on your body, take steps to deepen your direct individual research one plant at a time, until you are absolutely confident in using them. Here are some of the ingredients we like to use; use any of the following, alone or in combination, either dried or freshly picked.

BLADDERWRACK (SEAWEED) Supports balanced thyroid functioning; great source of iodine. Soothes and relieves digestive problems.

BURDOCK (LEAF AND ROOT) Rich in iron. Natural diuretic and liver detoxifier. Improves blood sugar levels. Aids in healing the skin, reduces inflammation, purifies the blood, strengthens the lymphatic system.

CHAGA (MUSHROOM) Anti-inflammatory and with soothing properties that aid a broad spectrum of irritations. Helps boost the immune system, regulates blood sugar.

CHAMOMILE (FLOWER) Reduces anxiety and stress. Anti-inflammatory and pain-reliever, especially that of the stomach. Known to promote digestive health and quality of sleep.

DANDELION (LEAF AND ROOT) Cooling for the body, cleanses and detoxifies the liver.

ELDER (BERRIES AND FLOWERS) Most commonly used to prevent and treat cold and flu symptoms. Anti-inflammatory to help skin, joint pain and swelling. Reduces swelling of the sinuses, relieves constipation. A natural diuretic.

FENNEL (SEED) Helps regulate blood pressure, supports good eyesight, helps purify blood.

HAWTHORN (LEAF, FLOWERS AND BERRIES) Prominently used for strengthening of the heart and circulatory system. Helps reduce anxiety and supports optimum functioning of the digestive system.

HEMP (THE WHOLE PLANT) Known to reduce chronic pain, alleviate anxiety and depression and promote heart health.

HOPS (FLOWER) Relaxes and soothes muscles, improves digestive system, helps improve sleep and treats insomnia.

HORSETAIL (LEAF) Soothes urinary tract infections. Aids and repairs hair, nails and skin. Fortifies immune system.

LAVENDER (FLOWER) Relaxes and soothes muscles, reduces nervousness and anxiety, helps improve sleep and treats insomnia. Lavender is also an excellent anti-inflammatory and antiseptic.

LINDEN BLOSSOM (FLOWER) Improves digestion. Fights infections by boosting the immune system. Rejuvenates skin, due to high levels of vitamin C, flavonoids and antioxidants. Can help stabilise weight fluctuations. Promotes heart health.

NETTLE (LEAF AND ROOT) Supports healthy joints and urinary system. Rich in iron, strengthens blood, gives a natural energy boost.

REISHI (MUSHROOM) Helps promote healthy heart, boosts immune system, promotes longevity, regulates blood sugar.

ROSEHIPS (FRUIT) High levels of vitamin C. Strengthens digestive and immune systems, an all-round tonic and a mood booster.

SEA BUCKTHORN (FRUIT) Rich in protein-building amino acids, folic acid and omega 3, 6, 7, 9. Balances blood sugar, aids wound healing and supports healthy brain and nervous system functions.

If you are interested in sourcing medicinal herbs from further afield, here are a few of our favourites:

BAOBAB (FRUIT) Very rich in vitamin C, this sour fruit native to Africa most often comes in a powder form. Great for strengthening the immune system. Antimicrobial, anti-viral, anti-inflammatory.

CATS CLAW (BARK) Native to the Amazon. Anti-inflammatory, especially linked with gastrointestinal functions. Aids in general digestive health and boosts immunity.

CHANCA PIEDRA (LEAF) Native to the Amazon and other tropical regions, cleanses and supports healthy liver function, helps clear kidney stones, strengthens digestion, purifies the bladder and kidneys.

GOJI BERRIES (FRUIT) Excellent source of antioxidants, boosts energy levels and supports a healthy immune system.

IRISH MOSS (SEAWEED) Native to most ocean coastlines. Helps with a wide spectrum of conditions. Supports positive emotional and mental health. Good source of sulphur compounds as well as iodine, bromine and beta-carotene. High in calcium, iron, magnesium, manganese, phosphorus, selenium and zinc and most trace minerals.

MORINGA (LEAF) Native to South Asia, this 'miracle' tree is rich in iron, calcium, magnesium and vitamin A.

SHATAVARI (ROOT) A wild variety of asparagus root mostly used in Ayurvedic medicine in India. Often associated with women's health and is said to regulate hormonal health. Alleviates pain, supports great memory. It is cooling and calming.

SCHIZANDRA BERRIES (FRUIT) Native to China and commonly used in Traditional Chinese Medicine. Promotes youthfulness, normalises blood sugar and blood pressure, stimulates immune system. Contains all five flavours.

BASIC INVINCIBILITEA

● **Makes 3–5 litres
(5¼–8¾ pints/
12½–20 cups)**

Choose up to a dozen herbs and spices you are already very familiar with (see suggestions on pages 202/203). If you are not familiar with the herbs and spices, take steps to deepen your direct individual research one plant at the time.

Even though making a steeped tea infusion is simple and many of these plants are quite well-known, these are pretty much the most potent wild foods when we learn to use them in the right way for us in adequate quantities.

Put 0.5g per person per day of each herb (see page 203) into 1.5–2 litres (2¾–3½ pints/6–8 cups) of pure filtered water. Depending on the season you can add freshly harvested herbs into the mix. For instance, if you'd like to infuse enough herbs for 2 people to last 3 days you would need to add 3–6g of each herb.

Infuse over a low heat until the temperature of the brew reaches 65–80°C/149–176°F. Boiling the water changes and intensifies the flavours, rapidly extracting more bitter nutrients to the surface. When at the right temperature, pour the infusion through a chinois or muslin and enjoy right away with your choice of sweetener or refrigerate for later use.

To continue brewing the same herbs, add 1.5–2 litres (2¾–3½ pints/6–8 cups) of fresh water onto the brewed herbs, and either refrigerate for next time or brew right away. Rebrew (add 1–3g of Irish moss and 1–3g of the dried flowers of your choice) and repeat the process above until the herbs lose their flavour or the tea water becomes clear. You can blend the brewed herbs with a pinch of salt and some tea to extract the last of the goodness and then strain off any bits through a chinois or a nut milk bag.

The tea with herbs inside will keep in the fridge for up to 7 days. Strained and ready tea (without a sweetener) will keep in the fridge for up to 5 days.

CREAMY AND SWEET INVINCIBILITEA

Add one or all of the following per 500ml–1 litre (18–36fl oz/2–4 cups) of Basic Invincibilitea (see opposite page):

- 1 tbsp coconut oil
- 1 tbsp raw black sesame butter or tahini
- 1 tbsp raw nut or seed butter (e.g. Brazil nut butter)
- 25g (1oz) cacao paste

TO SWEETEN
add one or two of the following to taste:
- handful of dried fruit, such as figs, apricots or mulberries
- 2 tbsp yacon syrup, yacon powder or sweetener of your choice
- 1 tbsp mesquite
- 1 tbsp lucuma powder
- 8 drops liquid stevia
- 1 tbsp xylitol
- 1 tbsp coconut sugar
- 1 tbsp maple syrup
- 1 tbsp wildcrafted honey

● **Serves 2–4**

To serve, blend or stir the ingredients of your choice in to the Basic Invincibilitea and serve right away.

WILD WISDOM

The number one rule of herbalism is compliance. If you don't take the herbs they won't work, and in order to feel the effects of the herbs and get yourself into a successful rhythm and mastery of this you should commit to this practice for at least 30 days.

FULL CIRCLE: THE HEART OF LIFE

We find ourselves on the edge of the old world and at the beginning of the new one. There is ever more collective awareness of the issues – and the solutions – required to solve sometimes seemingly impossible global and local problems. To take initiative in every moment is to become a part of a positive, 'win-finity' solution. Not just to think of it, but to be it, the best way we can each moment. Pick up the litter when you see it and reduce the amount of rubbish you generate (after all, the natural eco-system doesn't create any). Make more informed and inspiring food choices. Take the initiative to help out whenever you can. Be an ever-more fully expressed human being. Be tenacious and persistent. Do not compromise. Simple actions are within our power.

Regardless of the food we eat and the ways we choose to nourish our bodies, we are naturally happiest and most fulfilled when we are fully engaged in being an intrinsic part of a thriving and dynamic community, family, humanity and environment. Connect more with your larger, diverse communities or start your own real-life gathering. Have greater appreciation of the wisdom of elders, connect to local groups and reactivate the living, pulsating web of real-people interactions that are grounded in good will, positive solutions and a healthy dose of playfulness and light-heartedness. Ask yourself: how can we contribute to bettering our local community and environment every day? Directly, through sharing our most radiant selves, our gifts and creativity; and indirectly, by what we focus on and consume on a daily basis.

The connection with the diversity of tribes and the whole human family brings meaning to our everyday life and motivates us to live in balance, joyfully serving, celebrating and appreciating our ever-growing and transforming global and local family.

Slowly but surely, we further our knowledge of how to thrive and fulfil our place in this dance. This means allowing all realities to flow, being open to all people, all truths, all ideas, all plants, all lifestyles, all cultures, all disciplines and systems of thought, all sciences, all religions, all worldviews, all philosophies.

Embrace unity in diversity within and beyond yourselves. More profoundly, see and experience yourselves as an intricate link within a vast web of humanity, the Earth and existence.

The sole reason for gaining more knowledge about all the aspects of our being and our wellbeing and diving into plant-based kitchen alchemy, is to provide us with more tools to navigate ourselves back from the peripheries of the compass – the sometimes disconnected edges of our experience – to the centre of our lives. Wherein lies our timeless presence, our wild essence, our innate joy and potency to be a deliberate co-creator and contributor to existence.

The Wild Wellbeing Compass – and all related environments, rituals and edibles – is our way (one of the many out there) to start building bridges to reach that wild essence that is beating in the same rhythm as the Earth and the cosmos, at the heart of life, at the centre of our human experience. It is a humble attempt to merge the two polarities of our existence: the modern and the timeless. Neither is better or worthier than the other. Only by understanding both and realising more and more the authentic ways in which these polarities integrate in our lives, can we start connecting the dots between the wild and the cultivated, the natural and the urban, the individual and the collective, the modern and the traditional. In the process of this creative, playful, investigative learning grounded in the paradoxical nature of life, we find our wholeness, thriving and happiness. We create so much new deliciousness in all recipes of our lives: in the kitchen, our work, our families, communities and beyond. We find our ever-changing, transforming, unique wild self in amidst the ever-bubbling soup of life. Us and the wild start sharing the same breath again.

May the wisdom of the wild guide us in all aspects of our journey.

Spread love everywhere you go.
Let no one ever come to you
without leaving happier.
MOTHER TERESA

USEFUL INFORMATION

EQUIPMENT

Many of the things listed here you will already have in your kitchen. Some of it may be unfamiliar and will seem expensive but depending on your level of interest they are worth the investment. And of course, the equipment is only as good as the continuous use of it. So if you do choose to go ahead and upgrade your kitchen, make sure you create delicious recipes, build skills and nourish yourself and your loved ones on a regular basis.

HANDS Raw food is very tactile, sensual and playful. Embrace giving your hands a central stage in raw food preparation. The food will taste authentic to you, will be full of your presence and your energetic medicine. It will empower you to become more playful and creative, and everyone will feel tangible benefits of deliciousness and the care that you put into it. Whether it is massaging kale, tossing a salad, squeezing lemons, grinding nuts or seeds by hand, rinsing seaweed or plucking the leaves of fresh herbs – the opportunities are endless. Plants are always inviting us to play and have fun.

PESTLE AND MORTAR Probably the first tool on Earth, it is how our ancestors used to prepare food. Whether it is opening nuts, making a quick pesto, or grinding food to various degrees – whenever we are making small portions of recipes for one or two people – we will opt to use mortar and pestle instead of a blender/food processor for an extra personal touch and extraordinary flavour freshness.

HIGH-SPEED BLENDER There are many available now, ranging hugely in price and quality (although the two are not always linked). Do your research and get the best blender you can afford, and remember that if you want to get an ultra-smooth result you might need to pass it through a chinois or nut milk bag. Some blenders now come with two blending jugs, a small one for making a quick smoothie to go and a bigger one for making bigger batches. We typically use a 2L blender jug for all recipes

JUICER There are various juicer options that will suit all budgets and requirements. A hand crank juicer requires elbow grease but can produce high-quality juices with a good yield, along with a good workout. They are capable of juicing green leafy vegetables, which is the most integral part of any juice and can be taken anywhere as they don't rely on a power source. Electric juicers vary massively in price but you'll also need to consider how long they take to juice, whether they handle leafy greens well and how difficult they are to clean. If you are not ready to invest in a juicer, use a blender to blend fruit and vegetables and strain through a nut milk bag to remove excess pulp.

FOOD PROCESSOR A good food processor is incredibly useful for making pestos and salsas, slicing and grating vegetables. Many of them now come with spiraliser attachments. As always, they vary hugely in price but a good one is worth the investment for the amount it will do for you.

KNIVES Always keep your kitchen knives sharp; you will find it easier to develop your knife skills and it's generally safer than trying to cut with blunt knives. Ceramic blades are a nice option and are particularly helpful in raw food preparation as the ceramic blade ensures that oxidisation-prone vegetables and fruits (such as lettuce, avocado or apple) don't brown. We have a few must-have knives in the kitchen: a small fruit paring knife, a small serrated knife (ideal for cutting fruits and veg like tomatoes), a large, well-sharpened chef's knife for general chopping and slicing and a cleaver for opening coconuts.

DEHYDRATOR A dehydrator preserves the enzymes because it can cook below a temperature of 42°C/107°F. It is one of the cornerstone tools of raw cuisine, as it preserves by extracting moisture out of dishes and intensifies flavours. It is by no means essential, however. If you don't have one, measure what the lowest temperature your oven will go down to with a kitchen thermometer. All the recipes listed in this book that require dehydration can be adapted in the fan-assisted oven on the lowest setting. To decide on the time required for each recipe, look to achieve the final texture listed in the recipe and adapt the timings to it.

MANDOLIN OR SPIRALISER This is a fun tool for making great textures in noodle and spaghetti-like forms from vegetables such as courgettes, carrots, squash and sweet potatoes. There are both manual and electric options. A mandolin consists of a very sharp blade and is always to be used with the manufacturer's safety recommendations if you love and want to keep your fingers intact.

OTHER USEFUL ITEMS

- Coffee or spice grinder
- Salad spinner
- Cake tin and cake rings
- Sushi mat
- Cheese cloth/muslin cloth
- Chinois, fine sieve, nut milk bag
- Vegetable peeler
- Scales
- Measuring cups and spoons
- Kitchen thermometer
- Sprouter

INGREDIENT GUIDE

AGAVE NECTAR A clear or golden-shaded liquid sweetener from the agave plant that's often used in raw food dessert preparation due to its translucent quality and mild flavour. We make sure to source good-quality raw agave nectar (organic blue agave nectar) with minimal processing involved, as there are a lot of low-quality high-fructose syrup alternatives labelled as agave nectar/syrup, and there is a certain degree of controversy surrounding the level of process involved in making this sweetener. We tend to not overuse this sweetener on a regular basis and err on a side of caution.

CACAO Most often comes in four different raw forms. Cacao paste is 100 per cent cacao liquor in a solid form – dark, creamy, bitter and rich in flavour. Cacao nibs are crushed-up shelled cacao beans and are known to be an excellent energy booster. Cacao butter is a clear butter that appears after the process of extracting oil from the cacao liquor. It is solid at room temperature and carries a lovely aroma of chocolate. Most often used in dessert making. Cacao powder is what remains when cacao liquor is processed into butter and powder.

COCONUT MILK This is a practical ingredient in desserts as well as savoury dishes that carry a lot of spices, such as curries. If you prefer not to use coconut milk/cream in your recipes the closest replacement would be to make a nut cream or use shop-bought plant-based cream of your choice.

COCONUT OIL (EXTRA VIRGIN) Great in raw dessert-making due to its setting temperature of 24°C (75°F), although you can replace it with cacao butter when making raw desserts. We also like to use it for cooking if required due to its comparatively high smoke point – again, you can substitute it for other cooking oils, such as rapeseed, sunflower or avocado oil. There is a lot of debate whether saturated fats naturally found in coconut oil are beneficial. Like with most foods, you will find both sides of the argument as well as supporting evidence and reports for both: pro and anti coconut oil. Our take on the whole coconut debate is: like anything, use in moderation, as part of a versatile diet, see if your body loves it (ours do!) and adjust the quantities if needed.

COCONUT PALM SUGAR Dried-up granules of a palm tree nectar. Coconut palm sugar is on a lower GI scale in comparison to other common sweeteners and brings lovely caramel-y flavours to dishes.

CREAMED COCONUT Creamed coconut is a butter made from dehydrated coconut chips. Solid at room temperature and liquid when heated, it is extremely useful for adding creaminess to drinks and setting desserts.

DULSE RED SEAWEED Can be used in a sprinkle form over salads. Goes well in recipes where red colour and pigment is required. Has a lovely mild flavour that tends to work well in salads, stews and even smoothies. Excellent source of iodine, high in vitamin B6 and C. Rich in iron, potassium and sodium.

GOLDEN ALGAE OIL This vegetarian supplement is made from golden algae rich in omega oils and DHA, usually found in fish.

HE-SHOU-WU (FO-TI) This is one of the most potent and revered adaptogens in the world of herbalism. Highly valued in Chinese herbalism as a tonic associated with longevity, beauty, supporting blood circulation, liver and kidneys. While not an essential ingredient in the kitchen, whenever we feel like an extra support to our bodies is required, we love adding the extract powder to chocolate smoothies due to its naturally woody, mild flavour that goes hand in hand with all things cacao or coffee.

HIJIKI One of our favourite seaweeds to add to various savoury dishes due to its complementary textures and easy-going flavour. Great in stews, and any rich sauces. As with all seaweeds, while consistency in daily or weekly consumption is beneficial, moderation is important as overconsumption can lead to thyroid imbalances.

HONEY (RAW) We use honey and other bee products very sparingly, and only from trusted sources of beekeepers that have adequate assurances of bee and ecological welfare taken into account. As a rule, these honeys are raw (unpasteurised) and artisanal (small batch). We do not use honey in hot beverages or in cooking as traditionally in Ayurveda it is considered that honey turns into poison with heat. From a scientific perspective, honey is the most enzyme-rich food, so it doesn't make sense to destroy the enzymes with heat and then consume the honey.

IRISH MOSS A whitish, translucent seaweed with a very mild, neutral flavour often used to thicken desserts and to add extra nutrients to drinks and smoothies. Find dry Irish moss in herbalist stores or online. To use, rehydrate overnight in water, drain and use, or make a paste by blending rehydrated Irish moss with water (2:1 ratio with water).

LUCUMA A species of fruit tree native to the Andean valleys of South America. Comes in a powder form and fulfils the role of a mild, creamy natural sweetener. It is a useful ingredient in raw desserts and smoothies. Rich in zinc, calcium, vitamin C and iron.

MACA Also known as Peruvian ginseng, maca is a root vegetable native to South America and has a malty, earthy, nutty flavour with a slight bitter edge, depending on the variety. It is known to support hormonal health and provide plenty of energy. Often used as a culinary, medicinal ingredient in desserts and smoothies.

MEDICINAL MUSHROOM COMPLEX POWDER Usually suggested as an optional ingredient, use this extracted powder form as a mix of medicinal mushrooms or any of the following stand-alone extracts: reishi, cordyceps, chaga, maitake, shiitake, tremella, turkey tail and lion's mane. Great as a coffee replacement, in teas, smoothies and to add an extra medicinal quality to desserts.

NUTRITIONAL YEAST Dry golden flakes often used as a quick way of adding a cheesy/umami flavour to a vast array of dishes and dressings. As it is a deactivated yeast it doesn't upset the body's natural bacteriological/yeast balance and usually comes with plenty of B-group vitamins (sometimes fortified with B12).

OLIVE OIL, (EXTRA VIRGIN) Olive oil is our favourite for salads, raw dips and other raw dishes. Whenever a recipe calls for olive oil, it denotes extra virgin olive oil. As all plastics are oil-soluble to some degree and all oils are sensitive and reactive to light, our preference is to buy olive oil (as well as other oils) in darkened glass, ceramic containers or tins whenever possible. We tend not to cook with olive oil as the smoke point of this oil is quite low and it loses all the richness of flavour of the raw unprocessed oil.

ORGANIC LIQUID TRACE MINERALS This is an optional ingredient we like adding to our juices and smoothies from time to time. It adds a nutritional benefit and, also, depending on the brand we are using, a nice yoghurt-like sourness to smoothies. Available online and in health food stores.

PHYSALIS BERRIES (GOLDEN/INCAN BERRIES) Incan berries are native to South America, where they have been a traditional source of food and medicine for centuries. These small, yellow/orange berries are found fresh in small packets in most supermarkets where they are known as physalis, contain high amounts of vitamins and protein. The dried variety contains thousands of small seeds within each berry. They are super tart and sweet and go incredibly well in smoothies and desserts. They can be replaced with sea buckthorn berries, sour cherries or fresh rosehips.

PINE POLLEN Pine pollen is the male spore of the pine tree. It has been used for thousands of years in Asia to boost energy, strengthen the immune system and balance hormone levels. Rich in protein, it is great in drinks, desserts and dressings.

PROBIOTIC CAPSULES, POWDER AND PASTES Whenever a recipe calls for probiotic capsules, be sure to empty them out and not use the capsules themselves. Probiotics can be dairy-derived as well as soil-based: be sure to check before buying.

SALT Wherever we use salt we use natural unprocessed sea salt in minimal amounts. We love to have a few different kinds in our pantry, and explore the uses of black salt, fleur de sel, Himalayan pink salt, etc. Whenever we can, we avoid using standard table salt, as it is heavily processed, harsh to our bodies, and stripped of all nutrients – there is a vast array of beneficial trace minerals found in unprocessed sea salt.

SEA BUCKTHORN This local superfood berry is packed with antioxidants, rich in vitamin C and contains omega 3, 6, 7 and 9. It is tart and sour in flavour and comes in deepest pigments of yellow, not unlike turmeric. It is available either frozen or as bottled juice (pasteurised or unpasteurised), as a dried berry or in powder form.

SEA PURSLANE Found in the wild estuaries in most of the areas of the Northern hemisphere, sea purslane is one of a very few land plants rich in DHA and EPA omega-3 fatty acids usually found in fish. Replace with any other aromatic green of your choice.

SPIRULINA AND CHLORELLA Contains high sources of protein, chlorophyll and trace minerals. These green powders are great additions to green juices and smoothies to bring out the colour and up the nutrients.

SUNFLOWER LECITHIN A natural emulsifier that helps bind water-based and fat-based ingredients to make drinks smoother and creamier. In a restaurant setting it's useful for ensuring the consistency of a drink's texture and appearance but you can leave it out; it will slightly affect the texture, but not the flavour, so don't worry too much if you don't have it in your pantry.

TAMARI A gluten-free version of soy sauce that enriches dishes with a wonderful umami flavour. We always ensure we get an organic, non-GMO brand of tamari. For a gluten- and soy-free alternative, use coconut aminos, made from the fermented 'sap' of coconut palms.

TOCOS RICE BRAN SOLUBLES An optional ingredient, this is a great-tasting bioactive source of essential fatty and amino acids with antioxidant properties. Tocos comes in a powder form and is made from the soluble portion of the hull of rice. Rich in vitamin E, it adds an absolutely amazing creaminess to anything and everything. We often use it in smoothies, lattes and desserts.

XYLITOL A low-GI powdery white sweetener derived from birch trees resembling white sugar, which makes it useful for not changing the colour of the recipes. Has a refreshing, cooling sensation.

YACON SYRUP A low-GI liquid sweetener made from a relative of the Jerusalem artichoke. It is also a pre-biotic food rich in fructo-oligosaccharides (FOS).

INDEX

ACKNOWLEDGEMENTS

JOEL AND AISTE

A very special thank you to our teacher, elder and dear friend Maestro Manuel Rufino: thank you so much for being by our side each step of the way, for the unconditional love, for the memory of the vision, and for all your guidance and support. Like Wow. We are forever grateful, humbled and inspired with the courage to walk this path as your students.

The elders, and shamanic indigenous cultures that we had the privilege of meeting, learning from and spending time with: Maestro Domingo Dias Porta, Tito La Rosa, Tata Pedro and Marina Cruz and the Mayan people of Lake Attitlan, Marakame Don Jose and the Huichol people of Wirikuta, Baba Mahakala and Sangha of the Himalayan traditions, the people of the native Druid and Celtic traditions. As well as all the pioneers, healers, artists, gardeners and doctors in the fields of wellbeing I have been lucky enough to apprentice with and carry forward the torches of their work.

Deepest gratitude to the sacred traditions of humanity and the great initiates of all ages that always inspire us and guide our way.

JOEL

I would like to thank the collective community of creative consciousness which I like to address as "The Almighty Alliance of All Allies".

My mum, Roda Gazdar and all of our mothers are the divine love made manifest: Thank you for you, your unconditional love, your devotion, your sacrifice, your care and your wisdom. Thank you to my grandma Bucha 'Betty' Guzder Mistry upon whose hundredth birthday we opened Wild Food Café. You make everything perfect! Thank you to my grandfather Jehangir, and to all our adventurous ancestors many who have travelled the world and kept the eternal flame alive. Thank you to my father Philip and his companion Lia, and my paternal grandparents and ancestors who courageously went through many challenges just so I could be present here and now.

AISTE

I would like to take this opportunity to express my deepest thanks to my parents Augute and Algirdas, my grandparents, my sister Giedre and brother Vytautas and their families. Sweet gratitude to my home land and all the places wild and beautiful that showed me the magic of life. To all of life's circumstances – and people – that brought me to here and now and inevitably contributed to this creation. Your names might not all be listed here, but you are in my heart.

JOEL AND AISTE

To Anja (and Nicholas) Saunders for stewarding the phenomena of Neal's Yard and giving us the best shot ever to open Wild Food Café, we are forever grateful.

To Virginia Gini Pappadakis, for a life of friendship, a wonderful co-creative adventure, partnership, mentorship and an immeasurable support. Thank you from the bottom of our hearts.

To Thet Min Tun Head Chef, culinary partner and dear brother who puts a genius twist of execution to our wild experiments and visions. To Guilli our brilliant sous chef from Brazil with a big smile, and the whole team of wild superstars, past and present, that shine bright and provide us all with delicious plant-based innovations and heart-felt service day in and day out.

Rebecca Page for being a wild cultural ambassador par excellence at Wild Food Café and beyond, for your friendship, dedication and for all the support in bringing this book to the world.

To all the guests and raving fans of Wild Food Cafe.

To all the students and alumni of The Wild Food Café School.

To all of our growers, foragers and suppliers including: Yun Hider, Ann, Gail, Andrew, Bridget, Nikki and Kayleigh at Tree Harvest, John and the whole team at Earth Natural Foods, Stein and Ellie at Brambletye, Adrian and Nathan at Wild Country Organics, Infinity foods, Plawhatch and Tablehurst Farms, Choice Organics, Organic Herb Trading Company, Sky & Kate at Immortal Foods, Kieran and Steven at Hybrid Herbs.

To Sam Jackson at Penguin and Ebury Press for being the first to come to us to write this book. To Sam Crisp at Ebury Press, Valeria Huerta and Olive Percival for being patient with us and being most excellent agents guiding us along the way. To Barbara San Jose and Gail Harland for supporting us with everything we required to test the recipes, take the photos and do the endless edits. Belma Mahmut from Re'Bel crystals for sharing your crystal medicine with us and the world.

Daniel Priestley and Rob Allen, for being such great friends and supporters of our vision.

David Thunder and Tabitha Spence, David and Shruti Whittington, Ben Hewitt, Steven Nicolaides, Matt Canale, Scott Ashby & Marcus Shewry for your operational wizardry, Bill & Sue Dunster and the team at Zed Factory and all those who have contributed to the co-creation of Wild Food Café's looks and feels.

To our superhero best friends from all four courners of the world: Kevin Nathaniel, Kira Goldy, Agnieszka & Marcin, Aneta Ptak, Agnieszka and Radek, Kyra and Sebastian, Jerry and Laura, Jerry and Ixchel, Chris and

Agata, Shola and AJ, Paulina and Bartek, Brooke & Aiden, Nicole & Adrian, Matt, Lisa, Mary & Artur Soltys, Chris & Asia, Marek, Tommy & Nina, Debra, Leona & Mike, Sara and Z, Aum and OmniLove, Vid, Ezrin, Magdalena, Alyona, Paul Auerbach, Kyle, Lazo, Dr. Khartar Khalsa, Zoe Hind and Chris Parks. – we love you so much.

JOEL

Last but not least, thank you the friends on my path for gifting me their support in the best education I could have, and the freedom to make and learn from my own mistakes, to all the friends and cultural creatives who initiated me on to my path, from a society who had forgotten these rites of passage, through unconventional means. Gilly Mason, Tara Perry, 'Happy Face', 'Avocado' Gilchrist, Ash, Sil, Pete, Daze, Jody and Cec, Anders, Cosmic Steve, Mark Sinclair and the crew, Camilla, Greg Sams, Dinaz, Stu, Irene, Philippa and Sequenci for letting me take the helm and have a magical streak of beginners luck in an amazing church.

For my old buddies who've stayed present, despite distance: Nick West and Tarek Haddad.

To Eugene Tsui and Elisabeth Montgomery for guiding my early eco-architectural explorations in the San Francisco Bay Area.

AISTE

Lastly, biggest thanks to Joel, my beloved husband, co-creator, partner and adventure buddy. I am in deep gratitude to our love, playfulness, patience, determination and vision that carried us through many sleepless nights bringing this creation to the world.

JOEL

With Wildest appreciation of my beloved companion and ineffable inspiration Aiste, for blessing me with you radiant presence and blazing love, I feel like the luckiest being ever.

To ALL of LIFE.

AHO!